IDA TARBELL
First of the
Muckrakers

WOMEN OF AMERICA
Milton Meltzer, Editor

SEA AND EARTH *The Life of Rachel Carson*
By Philip Sterling

TONGUE OF FLAME *The Life of Lydia Maria Child*
By Milton Meltzer

TO THE BARRICADES *The Anarchist Life of Emma Goldman*
By Alix Shulman

LABOR'S DEFIANT LADY *The Story of Mother Jones*
By Irving Werstein

QUEEN OF POPULISTS *The Story of Mary Elizabeth Lease*
By Richard Stiller

PROBING THE UNKNOWN *The Story of Dr. Florence Sabin*
By Mary Kay Phelan

MARGARET SANGER *Pioneer of Birth Control*
By Lawrence Lader and Milton Meltzer

SOMEBODY'S ANGEL CHILD *The Story of Bessie Smith*
By Carman Moore

THE SENATOR FROM MAINE *Margaret Chase Smith*
By Alice Fleming

IDA TARBELL *First of the Muckrakers*
By Alice Fleming

NEIGHBOR TO THE WORLD *The Story of Lillian Wald*
By Irvin Block

BY ALICE FLEMING

IDA TARBELL
First of the
Muckrakers

ILLUSTRATED WITH PHOTOGRAPHS

THOMAS Y. CROWELL COMPANY   New York

Manufactured in the United States of America
L.C. Card 76-139103
ISBN 0-690-42881-2

2   3   4   5   6   7   8   9   10

IDA TARBELL
First of the
Muckrakers

Chapter 1

In the fall of 1901 a tall, dark-haired woman named Ida Tarbell began writing a series of magazine articles about John D. Rockefeller's monopoly of America's oil industry. At the time she expected the series to be three or four installments long.

Instead *The History of the Standard Oil Company* ran in *McClure's Magazine* for eighteen installments and became a two-volume, 554-page book. It inspired a public outcry against corrupt business practices, launched a new type of crusading journalism—muckraking—and eventually led to the dissolution of Rockefeller's giant company by the United States Supreme Court.

Ida Tarbell, who is still famous for her exposé of corruption in the oil industry, grew up in the same northwest corner of Pennsylvania where the precious black liquid was discovered. She was born in Erie County on November 5, 1857. If her parents had had their way, however, Ida would have been born in Taylor County, Iowa.

Ida's father, Franklin Tarbell, was both a school-teacher and a skilled carpenter, but after his marriage to Esther McCullogh in 1856 he decided to become a farmer. The McCulloghs and the Tarbells had been among the first settlers in northwestern Pennsylvania. Frank and Esther, following their pioneer heritage, wanted to push even farther across the continent.

Iowa seemed like the best place. It was a new state and land was plentiful. An ambitious young man could earn a good living for himself out there. Leaving his wife at her parents' home in Erie County, Frank Tarbell started west. He planned to buy a farm and build a house in Iowa; Esther would join him as soon as it was finished.

The farm was bought and the house built, but before the Tarbells could move into it, their plans were shattered by the panic of 1857. People began selling stocks and taking their money out of the banks at a feverish rate. Before long the country was in the throes of an economic depression. Frank Tarbell couldn't afford to bring his wife out to Iowa. In fact, he didn't even have the price of his own railroad ticket back to Pennsylvania. He had to work his way across the country, teaching at various one-room schoolhouses along the way. By the time he returned to Erie County, his daughter, Ida Minerva, was over a year old.

A slender child with straight brown hair and solemn eyes, she stared with suspicion at the tall stranger who strode into her grandfather's house and swept her mother into his arms. When it was her turn to be hugged and kissed, Ida shook her head emphatically and refused to let go of her mother's skirts. "Go away, bad man!" she cried.

Frank Tarbell did go away soon after that, but not because of Ida's command. When he was a student at the Jamestown Academy, just across the state line in New York, he had spent his summers skippering a fleet of flatboats that carried freight down the Allegheny and Ohio rivers. Now he went to work on the riverboats again, and after one trip that took him as far as Louisville, Kentucky, started home with the price of the move to Iowa carefully tucked away in his pocket.

As he traveled back to Erie County, Frank Tarbell began to hear some exciting rumors. A man named Edwin Drake had drilled the world's first oil well near Titusville, Pennsylvania.

The news that petroleum was to be found in this barren section of the Keystone State came as no surprise to Frank Tarbell. Enterprising tradesmen had been skimming oil off the surface of streams for decades and selling it as medicine. A few of them had discovered that rock oil, as the crude petroleum was called, could be used for lubricating machinery, and once the impurities were removed, it also made an excellent fuel for lamps.

It was not hard to see the potential value of rock oil; the problem was how to produce it in large quantities. Finally a New York lawyer named George Bissell hit upon the idea of drilling for it. Bissell organized a company and sent one of its stockholders, Colonel Edwin Drake, out to Pennsylvania with instructions to build an oil well.

It took Drake months to assemble the tools and machinery to do the job, but the well was finally completed in August 1859. On its first day in operation it produced twenty-five barrels of oil and sent all the residents of Allegheny County scurrying out to lease tracts of land and start farming for oil on their own. The "black gold" was going to make them rich.

The shores of Oil Creek, where Colonel Drake had set up his drills, were only a few miles out of Frank Tarbell's way. He decided to stop off and see what all the excitement was about. He found the flatlands around Titusville dotted with oil wells. Their owners boasted of drilling as much as a hundred barrels a day.

Realizing at once that containers would be needed for the slimy liquid, Frank Tarbell decided that his talents as a carpenter might be put to good use here.

"How would you like to see a tank that could hold five hundred barrels of that stuff?" he said to one man who had set up a drill along the banks of a creek called Cherry Run.

The man looked impressed. "Show me a model that won't leak," he said, "and I'll give you an order."

Frank Tarbell built the model; the man liked it and gave him an order for a dozen more. In a few months the erstwhile farmer was running a thriving business at the mouth of Cherry Run. The house in Iowa was sold and a new house started beside the creek. In the fall of 1860 Frank Tarbell took his wife, daughter, and new baby son, William, across the Allegheny foothills to live in it.

Ida was not happy about the move. The flatlands were an ugly contrast to the rolling green fields of Erie County, and the small house her father had built was a shanty compared to her Grandfather McCullogh's comfortable Cape Cod farmhouse. Ida hated the big black derrick beside the front door and the stench of the slimy oil pits in the yard. She missed the kittens and ducks and baby lambs that had been her playmates on the farm. She also missed being petted and pampered by her grandparents. Before long, Ida decided that she had had enough of Cherry Run. She was going back to Grandma's.

Esther Tarbell seemed unperturbed by her daughter's announcement, and Ida, a determined scowl on her tiny face, set off across the valley. A few hundred yards from the house, she came to an embankment. It was a small slope, but to Ida it seemed as steep as a mountain. She studied it for a long time. Even if she could figure out some way to scale it, she was not at all sure that she would find Grandma's house on the other side.

By now the shadows of late afternoon were beginning to shroud the valley in darkness. The oil derricks loomed above her like hulking monsters, and Ida began to look longingly back at the friendly light in her mother's kitchen window. At last, she turned around and trudged toward home.

When Esther Tarbell opened her front door a few minutes later, she found a small girl sitting mournfully on the steps. "Why Ida," she exclaimed, "I thought you had gone to Grandma's."

The unhappy runaway shook her head. "I didn't know the way," she sighed.

"Very well," Mrs. Tarbell said calmly. "Come in and get your supper."

Life in the Oil Region grew more bearable as Ida became better acquainted with her father. At first she had resented the strange man who gave her orders in a gruff voice and monopolized her mother's attention. But Frank Tarbell soon won his daughter over. He had a dozen funny songs to sing to her, a dozen lively tunes to pick out on the metal Jew's harp he carried in his pocket. Ida also liked to hear the stories of his adventures as a riverboat captain. In those days America's rivers were the country's principal highways, and Frank Tarbell had seen everything in his travels—collisions and robberies, carnivals and revival meetings.

Ida made her father's shop her playroom. She loved the fresh smell of the newly planed wood and the soft piles of curly pine shavings on the floor. They were fun to roll around in or flop on for a nap. Sometimes she would try to find the longest and curliest of the shavings and drape them around her homespun skirt or tuck them in her hair to cover up her plain brown braids.

Ida would have enjoyed climbing on the oil derrick beside the house, but her mother had said no the first time she caught the little girl trying to hoist herself onto the lowest crosspiece. Ida next turned her attention to the creek that ran beside their door. There was a small footbridge only a few feet from the house, and Ida would stand on it by the hour looking down at the turbulent water. She was curious about the creek. Some things floated on it, she noticed, while others sank to the bottom.

Five-year-old Ida decided to make a scientific study of the creek. Sticks floated, so did pine shavings—but buttons, stones, and her mother's hairpins did not. Ida suddenly began to wonder which of the two categories her brother William belonged to. One day she dropped him into the water to find out. Ida's curiosity was satisfied when William, thanks to his long baby skirts, joined the category of things that floated. And thanks to his terrified screams, a workman at one of the nearby enginehouses jumped in and rescued him before he was swept downstream.

Business in Allegheny County was booming. Kerosene, refined from rock oil, had replaced whale oil in the nation's lamps; and although the Civil War seemed far away from the Pennsylvania oil fields, oil was also greasing the machines that kept the Union army supplied with uniforms and ammunition.

Business in the Oil Region was so good that

Frank and Esther Tarbell could soon afford to move out of the cramped cabin on the flatlands and into a larger home on the hillside above the valley. In the flatlands the grass and trees were coated with thick black grease and the only scenery was a grotesque array of derricks, enginehouses, and tanks. On the hill the land was too steep for drilling, so the grass was still fresh and green, and laurels and azaleas grew in abundance. It was easy to forget the grimy process that was going on in the valley below.

One April afternoon, as Ida was playing in the front yard of the new house, she caught sight of her father coming up the hill from his shop. Frank Tarbell was normally a cheerful man. Even at the end of an exhausting day, he would come home with a happy smile and a twinkle in his merry blue eyes. On this particular day, however, his shoulders drooped and his head was bowed. Ida knew at once that something was wrong. Her mother must have sensed it too. Before Father reached the front door, she was out on the steps. "Frank, Frank, what is it?" she cried, running down the hill to meet him.

Ida was too far away to hear his murmured reply, but she saw her mother bury her face in her apron and run back to the house in tears. Ida heard the news when she came in a few minutes later. President Abraham Lincoln had been shot in Washington.

At seven Ida was still too young to understand death, but a few years later she learned about it in her own family. Shortly after they moved to the house on the hill, Esther Tarbell gave birth to another daughter, Sarah, and about a year later, to another son, Franklin Sumner Tarbell, Jr.

Little Frankie inherited his father's sparkling blue eyes and sunny disposition, and he quickly became the darling of the family. Then one winter he was stricken with scarlet fever and died. Ida and her brother Will were as heartbroken as their parents. Only Sarah, who was the baby now, could not comprehend it. She wondered why Mother and Father wept over Frankie. "If they want to see him," she whispered to Ida, "why don't they put a ladder from the top of the hill up to the sky into heaven and climb up? If Frankie is there, God will let them see him."

Iron oil tanks were gradually replacing wooden ones, so Frank Tarbell closed up his shop at Cherry Run and went into business as an oil producer. His partner was a man named Hess, who had his own wells on another oil farm several miles across the hills. Mr. Hess had a daughter who was the same age as Ida and also bore the same name. The two Idas became fast friends and visited back and forth whenever their fathers got together on business.

Ida was always happy to see Mr. Hess come riding up to their door. After conferring with her father and enjoying one of her mother's chicken dinners, he would saddle up his horses, High Fly and Shoo Fly, and trot off across the hills with his partner's daughter beside him. Along the way Mr. Hess would show her the stars.

"There's Orion, the Hunter," he'd say, tracing the constellation with his finger. "See the three bright stars in his belt."

Ida had never known anything about the stars, but she soon learned the constellations and their legends by heart.

As Frank Tarbell's income increased, his family's style of living began to improve too. An ornately carved square piano appeared in the parlor, and Ida was put to work learning scales and arpeggios. The works of Shakespeare and Sir Walter Scott, handsomely bound in leather, became the nucleus of a family library. Father also began to subscribe to the *New York Tribune* and to magazines like *Harper's Weekly* and *Harper's Monthly*.

Ida and her brother Will became avid readers. They would lie for hours stretched out on their stomachs, their legs in the air, poring over the *Weekly*'s special issues on the Civil War. They were both too young to remember the bloody conflict, but now, through the pages of the magazine, they traced its history from the opening shots at Fort Sumter to the final surrender at Appomattox.

On warm spring days Ida would pack a lunch for herself and spend the afternoon in the woods. Tucked into the picnic basket beside her sandwich and jug of lemonade, there would invariably be a copy of the *Monthly* with a story by Charles Dickens or William Thackeray that she was anxious to enjoy.

Ida's solitary picnics were impromptu affairs, but

when the whole family went picnicking the preparations took several days. The menu was always the same—veal loaf, cold tongue, hard-boiled eggs, spiced peaches, pickles, buttered rusks, and jelly. For dessert Esther Tarbell made cookies, doughnuts, and a chocolate cake. Ida and Sarah helped their mother get out the tin cups and plates and pack the big wicker baskets. By the time they were ready to leave, Frank Tarbell used to vow that they had enough food to last them for a month.

The family's favorite excursion was to Lake Chautauqua, fifty miles away in southwestern New York State. They would take the train to a pretty resort town called Mayville. From there a small white steamer chugged up and down to Jamestown, twenty miles away at the opposite end of the lake. The Tarbells would unpack their picnic baskets and eat their lunch on the upper deck of the steamer.

By the time the boat docked at Jamestown, Ida, Will, and Sarah would invariably complain of being thirsty. Father's reaction was always the same. "If you're thirsty," he would say with a perfectly straight face, "there's a pump near the town dock where we can get a drink of water."

Father knew very well that it wasn't a drink of water they wanted at all. After a few more minutes of teasing he would march them all uptown for a bottle of sarsparilla or cherry pop. There was just enough time to finish their sodas and get back to the boat before the whistle blew. Then they would head back to Mayville to catch the evening train home.

The area around Cherry Run where the Tarbells lived soon grew into a town and was given the name of Rouseville. Dance halls and saloons lined the main streets of most of the towns in the oil region, but the residents of Rouseville were anxious to make it a decent place in which to raise a family.

One of the best ways to bring order into the community, they decided, was by establishing a church. Frank Tarbell helped raise the money to build it, and he and his wife were among its staunchest members. They saw to it that their children attended Sunday school and Wednesday night prayer meetings, and once, when a revival meeting came to town, they took them to that as well. Ida was wide-eyed at the preacher's descriptions of the terrible punishments that God had in store for sinners. When he called on everyone in the congregation to repent of their evil ways and be saved, she saw several of her friends stand up and approach the altar. Ida immediately jumped up and joined them.

Although she was extremely proud of her piety that evening, the repentant sinner soon began to have second thoughts about it. She knew she had not gone to the altar in a spirit of prayer but simply because everyone else was doing it. Moreover, all the time she was kneeling there, supposedly in remorse for her sins, she had actually been wondering if the rest of the congregation was noticing her new cream-colored coat and the lovely crimson ribbons on her hat.

Ida had not considered herself a sinner before the

revival meeting, but she was convinced that she was one now. She lay awake nights accusing herself of vanity and hypocrisy. She never confessed her guilt, even to her good friend, Ida Hess, but it made her think very seriously about the difference between how she had acted and what she had really thought. She wondered if other people were insincere sometimes too.

Ida's pangs of conscience eventually disappeared, but then she became preoccupied with another problem. For weeks there had been whispered conferences between her mother and father. Ida suspected that something was going on, and finally, one evening, Frank Tarbell put down his napkin, pushed back his chair from the dinner table, and said, "How would you like to move to Titusville?"

Ida was stunned at the thought of leaving Rouseville. She knew every floorboard in the house, every tree and shrub on the hillside. She could not imagine living anywhere else. But Frank and Esther Tarbell were convinced that Ida and Will and Sarah would be better off in Titusville. They would have a nicer house, better schools, and more friends to play with. The decision was already made.

"We'll be leaving at the end of the month," Father said.

Chapter 2

Unlike many cities in the oil region, Titusville had managed to grow larger and richer without losing its dignity and sense of order. Fine homes flanked the quiet tree-lined streets, churches and schools were being built to accommodate the steadily growing population, and a new opera house was rising in a vacant lot downtown. Although Ida was still not sure she was going to like it there, she was forced to admit that the new house her father built for them was far more impressive than the one they had lived in in Rouseville.

A few years after the Tarbells settled near Cherry Run, a new vein of oil was discovered less than a dozen miles away. The area, which was called Pithole, developed almost overnight into a bustling town of twenty thousand people. Then, in 1865, the wells abruptly dried up, the oilmen moved on, and Pithole became a ghost town.

During its brief period of prosperity Pithole had

been large enough to support several hotels. One of them, the Bonta House, had tall French windows, spacious verandahs, and a majestic tower above its entrance. The Bonta House had cost more than $60,000 to build. After the Pithole disaster, Frank Tarbell bought it for $600. The hotel, tower and all, was carefully taken down, loaded onto several vans, and carted the ten miles to Titusville. There Frank Tarbell reassembled it for his family to live in.

Ida loved the iron grillwork trim on the outside and the carved wood moldings on the inside, but her favorite spot in the hotel-turned-house was the tower room. She often climbed the winding staircase to sit by the big double windows and gaze out on the town below her.

Ida might have been happy in Titusville, but her initial distrust of the move was confirmed as soon as she started school. In Rouseville she had gone to a private school. There were only five or six pupils in the class and the teacher treated each of them like a personal friend. In Titusville Ida found herself in a classroom with thirty-five other boys and girls. The teacher barely noticed her. In fact, Ida was not even certain she knew her name.

From first grade to seventh grade, Ida had rarely missed a day of school. Now, in eighth grade, unable to endure her anonymous existence, she began to be absent more and more. She would leave the house at the usual time in the morning, but instead of walking the few short blocks to the red brick schoolhouse, she would slip off down a side street and spend the day alone in the woods.

It was far more interesting than going to school. Sometimes she brought along a book to read. More often, she was content to collect rocks or wild flowers, or study the squirrels and rabbits that darted in and out among the trees.

Playing hooky soon became a regular habit with Ida. Her mother assumed that she was going to school, and her teacher, as far as she could tell, assumed she was staying home with a stomach ache or cold. Then one day Ida discovered that the teacher had been paying more attention to her than she suspected.

"Miss Tarbell," the woman said one morning. "You were absent yesterday for the seventh time this term."

Ida could feel her cheeks burn with shame. She started to murmur something about being sick, but before she could get the first words out the teacher launched into a scathing lecture on truancy. Ida sank lower and lower in her seat, wishing she could disappear behind the map of the United States that hung on the wall beside her.

When the teacher finally finished her scolding and began the arithmetic lesson for the day, Ida sat silent and red-faced. She had been humiliated by the teacher's lecture, but as the day wore on her humiliation began to give way to anger. It was not the teacher she was angry at, it was herself.

Ida's mother often spoke with pride of her family.

She was descended from a long list of distinguished ancestors that dated back to Sir Walter Raleigh and included Samuel Seabury, the first Episcopal bishop of the United States. The mortified eighth-grader was certain that she was going to be remembered as the black sheep of the bunch. That morning she resolved to mend her ways.

Ida stuck to her resolve, and by the time school closed in June she not only had a perfect attendance record, but her name was at the top of the honor roll.

Ida continued to lead her class at Titusville High School, but although she was an expert at solving algebra problems and translating sentences into Latin, she regarded her schoolwork as a game. As far as she could see, it had very little relation to her daily life. Then one day she came across some textbooks in the school library. She was totally unfamiliar with the subjects—zoology, geology, and botany. Ida turned the pages with a breathless sense of discovery. The books were about things she understood and loved —plants, rocks, animals, insects. She had been studying them for as long as she could remember without ever realizing that they were taught in school.

Ida's bedroom shelves were full of pressed leaves, jars of spiders and lizards, and butterflies she had caught and preserved under glass. She knew them by their common names, but according to the textbooks they also had scientific labels, Latin names that were longer and much harder to remember. Ida made up her mind to learn them by heart.

Busy with her schoolwork and absorbed by her interest in science, Ida quickly forgot that she had ever complained about moving to Titusville. Her father's income continued to increase and his success was reflected in his family's style of living. There were several horses in the backyard stable, including a small white mare especially for Ida.

On New Year's Day, when all the ladies in Titusville held open house, Esther Tarbell received her guests in a stylish gown. A pair of hired girls in starched white aprons were kept busy filling the crystal punch bowl and replenishing the cold meats and salads on the silver platters in the dining room.

But the biggest improvement, as far as Ida was concerned, was Christmas. Will and Sarah were too young to remember the lean years in the cabin on the flatlands. There had been only a scraggly Christmas tree then, and walnuts and peppermints had taken the place of presents. Ida had sulked and asked why she didn't get real gifts like the children in the books she had read.

Esther Tarbell had tried to explain that it was not the presents that counted, but the spirit of love in which they were given. The little girl was too young to understand. Frank Tarbell would pat her small head lovingly and promise that someday their Christmases would be as wonderful as they were in the storybooks. "Just wait, pussycat," he would tell her. "Just wait."

When the Tarbells left the cabin and moved to the house on the hill, there were a few more presents under the Christmas tree, but it was not until they settled in Titusville that Father's promise really came true.

Ida came downstairs on Christmas morning to find an enormous evergreen tree scraping the ceiling in the parlor. The same angel that had adorned the scrawny Christmas trees in the flatlands was perched on top, but the rest of the decorations were completely new. Fat red and silver balls hung from the branches, feathery imitations of birds perched on the limbs, and ropes of tinsel wended their way in between the candy canes and gingerbread men.

Will and Sarah had already pounced on their gifts, and the parlor resounded with exclamations of astonishment and delight. Will had a set of shiny trains. Sarah had a doll house that was almost as tall as she was. Ida was too old for toys. Her gift was a dark green velvet cape with a bonnet and muff to match.

She put it on and danced out to admire herself in the big gilt-edged mirror in the downstairs hall. Her mother, who had received a coat of soft black sealskin, rushed out and stood beside her. The two of them giggled with delight. "Oh Papa," Ida gasped, dashing back into the parlor and giving her father a grateful hug, "this is a Christmas I'll never forget!"

The nation continued to buy petroleum at an astounding rate, and the wells in Oil Creek Valley continued to produce it. Lumber, machinery, and men were needed to keep them going. Soon railroad tracks came through Titusville and trains began running on a regular schedule to Cleveland, Pittsburgh, and Philadelphia. The producers in Oil Creek Valley used the railroads to ship their crude oil out of the region for refining. It seemed like an ideal method of transportation, but one day the system was threatened in a rather unexpected way.

A small group of Cleveland oil refiners formed an organization which they called the South Improvement Company. They persuaded the railroads to allow them to send and receive their oil at lower rates and to charge higher rates to companies that were not in the organization. The agreement was designed to force competing oil refiners out of business. After that, the South Improvement Company would have a monopoly. They could set the price of crude oil at whatever figure they wished.

When the rate increase was announced in the newspapers on February 26, 1872, it sent every man in the Oil Region into a frenzy. They were not angry at the railroads—they had always been notorious for their dishonesty. But they were furious to find such double-dealing among their fellow oilmen.

The day after the news appeared in the morning papers, three thousand angry men gathered for a protest meeting at the Titusville Opera House. They were drillers, pumpers, producers, and refiners, and they carried banners proclaiming "Down with the conspirators!" and "No compromise!"

Calling themselves the Petroleum Producers'

Union, the men launched a full-scale attack against the South Improvement Company. They asked the state legislature to revoke its license to operate in Pennsylvania, they sent a petition to Congress demanding an investigation of both the company and the railroads, and they drew up a list of the conspirators and sent it to every prominent businessman and lawmaker in the country so that the "enemies of freedom of trade may be known and shunned by all honest men."

The mastermind of the conspiracy was a man named John D. Rockefeller, who was head of the Standard Oil Company. Frank Tarbell and the other men in Oil Creek Valley signed a pledge never to ship their oil to Rockefeller's company for refining.

There were meetings at the Opera House almost every night to denounce Rockefeller's scheme. Not content with orderly protest, a few men decided to take matters into their own hands. They slipped out of town one evening and assembled in the bushes along the railroad tracks. As the train carrying oil for the South Improvement Company came chugging toward their hideaway, several of the men stepped forward and flagged it down. While the ringleaders held the engineer and the fireman hostage, the rest of the men rushed to the tank cars, unscrewed their caps, and let the oil drain out on the tracks.

The citizens of Oil Creek Valley caused such an uproar over the South Improvement Company that the railroads eventually backed out of their contract and signed an agreement guaranteeing the same rates to everyone who used their lines.

The Tarbell household had been unbelievably somber during the long weeks it had taken to settle the matter. Frank Tarbell was too preoccupied to sing or play his Jew's harp. Even his customary after-dinner cigar failed to erase the worried frown from his face.

Ida found it hard to follow her parents' conversations about monopolies and privileges, and one day she asked her father to tell her in simple language what the trouble was all about.

"It's as if you were riding along on that little white horse of yours," Frank Tarbell said, "and someone tried to crowd you off the road."

Ida nodded.

"The railroads run through Titusville by the consent of the people who live here," her father continued. "Now they are ignoring the general public and giving special privileges to a small handful of men. It isn't fair."

Ida was appalled to discover that John D. Rockefeller was not the only man in the country who was becoming rich by ignoring the rights of others. Her father ticked off a whole list of "robber barons," as the powerful industrialists would one day be called. There was Andrew Carnegie, who was on his way to dominating the steel industry; J. P. Morgan, the New York banker; and a whole group of men like

James Hill, Edward Harriman, Jay Gould, and Cornelius Vanderbilt, who controlled the nation's railroads.

Ida, who had an inherent respect for justice, was as indignant as her father at some of their tactics. She vowed that if she ever had a chance, she would do something to make the world aware of the evils of dishonesty and greed.

When the dispute was settled, her vow was quickly forgotten. For the present, at least, Ida was completely absorbed with science. Her fascination for the subject started her browsing in her father's library. She found several books there on the formation of the earth, but the more she read, the more upset she became. One of the books, Charles Darwin's *Origin of Species,* suggested that instead of being created by God in six days, as the Book of Genesis described it, the world had actually taken millions of years to evolve.

Darwin's theory of evolution was causing a tremendous controversy in the Christian church at the time. Ida found herself caught up in it in a very personal way. She had been taught to believe in God and the Bible, but it was difficult to reconcile her religious beliefs with what she was learning about science. She felt confused and frightened and wondered desperately where she could turn for guidance.

The answer came to her one day when she started to think about the word evolution. If things grew, they had to start from somewhere. If only she could find out where, Ida was sure she could find her way back to God.

The first requirement for Ida's investigations into the origin of nature was a microscope. She bought one with money she had received for Christmas and birthday presents. Mother let her turn the tower room into a laboratory, and after that Ida spent more time than ever in her aerie.

The microscope did not solve her doubts about the Book of Genesis but it did help her decide on a career. She was never going to marry. Instead, she was going to get a college degree and go on to become a microscopist in a real scientific laboratory.

Chapter 3

In the nineteenth century it was unusual for a girl to go to college. Most parents believed that too much education would endanger their daughters' health and, equally frightening, ruin their chances for marriage. Frank and Esther Tarbell were more broadminded. If Ida had her heart set on a college education, they saw no reason to stand in her way.

The college Ida decided on was Cornell, but a few weeks before she was to begin her freshman year, the president of Allegheny College, Dr. Lucius Bugbee, came to visit her parents. Inevitably the dinner table conversation got around to education. When Dr. Bugbee discovered that Ida was enrolled at Cornell, he raised his hands in mock dismay. "What's wrong with Allegheny?" he demanded.

Lucius Bugbee had a long list of reasons why Ida should give up Cornell and come to Allegheny instead. "It's closer to home," he told her, "and it's supported by your own Methodist religion."

When Ida still looked dubious, he dredged up a fresh set of arguments. Allegheny was more advanced than Cornell. It had opened its doors to women a full two years earlier. Besides, Ida was a pioneer. It was her duty to further the cause of higher education for women in her own home state.

Ida, who felt no special commitment to either school, laughingly conceded that Dr. Bugbee was a persuasive man. By the time his visit was over, she was enrolled in Allegheny College.

The school was in a town called Meadville about thirty miles from home. The place came as a complete surprise to Ida. In the Oil Region everything was just being discovered or just being built. Meadville had a tradition that dated back over a hundred years. It was Ida's first contact with history.

The town was built along the banks of French Creek, one of the tributaries of the Allegheny River. George Washington had passed through it in 1753 on his way to Fort Duquesne—the present city of Pittsburgh. According to legend, the future Father of his Country had stopped to drink at a spring near the edge of the Allegheny campus.

Soon after that, a number of settlers, led by a man named David Mead, arrived in the area. One of the first things they wanted for their new town was a college. They invited a New England clergyman and educator, Timothy Alden, out to organize one. For three years the school's only headquarters was in Meadville's log courthouse. Finally, in 1820, Alden raised enough money to begin construction of the college's first building, Bentley Hall.

When Ida Tarbell arrived on the campus fifty-six years later, she stared with amazement at Bentley Hall. Next to Independence Hall, it was the most perfect example of Colonial architecture in the state of Pennsylvania. Ida, who had grown up amidst jerry-built cabins and cluttered Victorian houses, was speechless. It was the first classically beautiful building she had ever seen.

Allegheny College had become coeducational in 1870, but so far there had been no rush of girls to apply. Only ten women had been graduated in the six years before Ida got there. When she arrived in 1876, there were two women seniors, two juniors, and no sophomores. In the freshman class, she was the lone girl among forty not very friendly boys.

Ida was enrolled in the natural science department, which was headed by a lively, cheerful man named Jeremiah Tingley. Professor Tingley encouraged her to use her microscope constantly and also urged her to experiment with some of the other more complicated instruments in the college laboratory. After classes he would frequently invite her to have tea with him and his wife. The Tingleys had a comfortable, book-lined apartment in one wing of Bentley Hall. They had both traveled and read widely, and Ida thoroughly enjoyed her visits with them.

Jeremiah Tingley followed every new discovery

in the field of science. Soon after she started college, Ida had taken a few days off to visit the International Centennial Exposition in Philadelphia with her father. When she returned to Meadville, Professor Tingley's first question was, "Did you see the telephone?"

Ida had spent most of her time gaping at two exhibits—a Corot painting and a model of a steam engine. She had to confess that she hadn't even heard of the telephone. She was baffled by Professor Tingley's disappointment until, a few weeks later, he gave the class a lecture on Alexander Graham Bell's remarkable new invention. "You'll talk to your homes from these rooms one day," he predicted. "New York will talk to Boston."

It sounded incredible, but Ida, who respected Jeremiah Tingley's opinion, believed him. One of the boys in the class, however, was more skeptical. "Dreamer," Ida heard him mutter behind her.

Professor Tingley's eagerness to investigate new discoveries taught Ida the power of enthusiasm. Her Latin professor, George Haskins, gave her an equally valuable lesson. He taught her to appreciate contempt.

The Tarbell household had a gentle atmosphere. Criticism was avoided and personal feelings spared. If the truth hurt, it was concealed by a white lie. Professor Haskins had no such code. He expected his students to be serious-minded and diligent. Those who were not were treated with contempt and sarcasm.

It was a devastating experience to earn George Haskins' disapproval but it was also an enlightening one. His scathing remarks taught Ida to work steadily and with discipline, not to waste her time, and not to give up until she had accomplished the task she set out to do.

There were times during Ida's four years at Allegheny when she was grateful for her pioneer upbringing. Bentley Hall was beautiful from the outside, but the inside was not particularly comfortable. The building's classrooms were furnished with hard wood chairs and illuminated with kerosene lamps. Potbellied cast-iron stoves provided the only heat. It was never enough. Bentley Hall was miserably chilly all winter long, and when it snowed the students tracked the snow in on their boots and the floors became wet as well as cold. Ida often wore her muffler both indoors and out.

Among the many pleasant discoveries of Ida's four years at college were boys. Except for her brother Will and his friends, she had had little contact with the opposite sex. In Titusville the only activities that brought boys and girls together were dances and parlor games. Ida's Methodist upbringing forbade dancing, and she was neither interested in, nor good at, games. Her social life was confined to strolling up and down Main Street on Saturday evening with one of her girl friends.

At college there were many more opportunities for sociability. The boys in the freshman class, hostile or indifferent at first, gradually grew more relaxed in feminine company. They were particularly fond of Ida, who, at twenty, had developed into a slim, straight-shouldered young lady with dark eyes, fair skin, and soft brown hair. She was by no means the beauty of the college, but her honest smile and her pleasant manner won her many friends.

Allegheny had a number of Greek letter fraternities. It was customary for the boys who belonged to them to give their fraternity pins to the girls they liked best. The girls were then pledged to date only the members of that particular fraternity. Ida resented the custom. She didn't want to be labeled a Delta girl or a Gamma girl; she wanted to choose her friends from any fraternity she pleased.

Ignoring the unwritten rule, Ida accepted four pins from four boys in her class. All of them belonged to different fraternities. There was considerable consternation in chapel when she appeared one morning wearing the pins on the front of her coat. The boys in all four fraternities snubbed her for weeks. Ida didn't mind. She still had plenty of non-fraternity friends.

Ida had entered college with two ambitions—to learn everything she could about science and to make herself financially independent. She had done her best to realize the first ambition, and by the time she graduated in 1880 she was on her way to realizing the second. The Poland Union Seminary in Poland, Ohio, had asked her to become its preceptress, or headmistress, at a salary of $500 a year. Ida accepted at once. She did not want to become a teacher, but the sum sounded so generous that she could probably save enough to pay for graduate studies in science.

Poland, Ohio, was a quiet place. No railroads or oil wells disturbed its rural serenity. The town's sole industry was the seminary. It offered both high school and college subjects and was the only educational institution for miles around.

School hadn't even started, however, before Ida began to have doubts about her new position. Miss Blakely, the woman she succeeded as preceptress, had been at the seminary for years. She was loved and admired by everyone in town.

Ida had no sooner arrived in Poland than people began stopping her on the street. "So it's you that's taking Miss Blakely's place," they would say. "You have no idea how badly we feel about her resigning. She was a wonderful teacher, a beautiful character."

Then they would eye Miss Blakely's youthful successor suspiciously and add, "You look pretty young; you haven't had much experience, have you?"

It was bad enough to be constantly compared to her predecessor, but on top of that, Ida also had to put up with a difficult schedule. Besides running the school, she taught eight subjects—Greek, Latin, French, German, geology, botany, geometry, and trigonometry. It was an exhausting job, but Ida, who was determined to do well, never thought to complain.

The new preceptress had no trouble with her regular classes, but there were two extra courses that almost drove her to despair. One was called Verb Grammar; the other, Percentage Arithmetic. They received their names from the sections of the textbooks where the term's work began.

The courses were given for the schoolteachers in the area who returned to the seminary from time to time to brush up on their teaching techniques. Each year the two subjects they requested without fail were Verb Grammar and Percentage Arithmetic.

The teachers were a great trial to Ida. They were all older and more experienced than she was and they didn't hesitate to let her know it. Moreover, they seemed to know both subjects inside out. Ida had not studied either of them since her grammar school days.

She grew to dread the two classes and more than once awoke in the middle of the night trembling with fear. Then one day a man named Robert Walker, who was the local banker and one of the most respected men in town, came up to her on the street. "Sis," he said, "you are following a fine teacher."

Ida smiled weakly. She had heard the remark a hundred times before. But Mr. Walker had something more to tell her. "Don't worry," he said with an encouraging wink. "What you must do is keep a stiff upper lip."

It was the first time anyone in Poland had given Ida any sympathy. She went home determined to survive her two-year term as preceptress. With a little luck, she might even find a way to conquer Verb Grammar and Percentage Arithmetic.

Not long after her encounter with Robert Walker, Ida suddenly realized something. She had often wondered why her teacher-students insisted on taking the same two courses over and over again. Then one day it dawned on her that they did not really understand the work. They had memorized the answers and they came to the seminary each year to refresh their memories.

Ida decided to present them with some problems and sentences they had never seen before. She selected them from textbooks that she was sure they would not be familiar with. The next day she strolled nonchalantly into the classroom and put a few of the new problems on the blackboard.

Just as she had anticipated, the teachers had no idea how to solve them. They stared at each other in complete confusion until one young man finally raised his hand. He had always been one of the most obnoxious students in the class, but now he was cringingly polite. "Those examples aren't in our books," he whined.

"What difference does that make?" the preceptress replied innocently. "The only important thing is that you know the principles. Once you know them and can apply them, it doesn't matter what examples you do."

The teachers' smugness evaporated as if by magic, and they meekly settled down to learn at last what they had been teaching for years. Ida, watching them, found it hard to conceal a triumphant smile.

Chapter 4

At times, Ida felt that the conquests of Verb Grammar and Percentage Arithmetic were her only accomplishments at Poland Union Seminary.

She had looked on the job of preceptress as a stepping-stone to a more rewarding career in science. She had even brought her beloved microscope with her to Poland but she had been much too busy to use it. Her plan to save enough money to continue her studies in graduate school had not worked out either. Somehow the $500-a-year salary seemed to disappear at an alarming rate.

By the time Ida paid her room and board and bought herself a dress or two to wear to school, there was very little left in her pay envelope. More than once, she had to write home to her father and ask him for some extra money to tide her over until the following month.

The one thing that made Poland bearable for Ida was her friendship with Clara Walker. Clara was the daughter of the banker who had stopped Ida on the street when she first came to town and urged her to keep a stiff upper lip. A few days after that, Clara drove up to the door of the seminary. When Ida came out, she invited her to go for a drive in her high-wheeled sulky. It was the second gesture of kindness that Ida had received in Poland, and she accepted Clara's offer with a grateful smile.

The two young women soon became close friends. They frequently went driving together after school and on weekends. Clara knew almost every square inch of Mahoning County. She showed Ida the enormous farms with their huge herds of cows and sheep. In some places the countryside was still as unspoiled as it had been when Ohio was settled. Elsewhere the rich farmlands were gradually giving way to factories and coal mines. America, once a nation of farmers and shopkeepers, was rapidly becoming a nation of manufacturers and businessmen.

Occasionally Clara and Ida would drive the ten miles into Youngstown for a concert or play. Ida always shuddered to see the ugly smokestacks and smelting furnaces that lined the road into the city. She knew that millworkers by the thousands were needed to man them and that they lived and worked in wretched conditions, while a small handful of millowners became multimillionaires.

Poland's preceptress had made up her mind to leave the seminary when her two-year contract expired. She had no idea how she would support herself after that, but she was certain it would not be as a teacher. In the spring of 1882 she wrote to her mother and asked if she could come back to Titusville.

"Of course," Esther Tarbell wrote back promptly. "This is your home. You're always welcome here."

Frank and Esther Tarbell continued to be active members of the Methodist church. Whenever a guest preacher came to town, he was invited to stay overnight in their home. Dr. Lucius Bugbee, the president of Allegheny College, had been the first such visitor to influence Ida's direction in life. Dr. Theodore Flood became the second. A retired minister, Dr. Flood was the editor of a magazine called *The Chautauquan*. He came to speak at a prayer meeting in Titusville, stayed with the Tarbells, and soon persuaded their daughter to join his staff.

The Chautauqua Movement, which had started a few years earlier, was to be a dominant force in American life until the beginning of the twentieth century. The movement began as a Methodist camp meeting that was held each summer at Fair Point on the shores of Lake Chautauqua. The Tarbells used to go there regularly all during Ida's high school and college years. Like the other families who attended, they slept in tents, ate their meals in a community mess hall, and took part in a daily schedule of church services and Bible classes.

Ida had happy memories of her vacations at Lake Chautauqua. Her father had a small, flat-bottomed boat which she delighted in punting about the lake. Another favorite sport among the younger summer residents was playing tag on the large relief map of the Holy Land that had been laid out along the shores of the lake. There were plaster of Paris models of the various towns built to scale. One of the rules of the game was that you could not be tagged if you stood next to Jerusalem.

The Chautauqua Assembly had been organized by an Ohio industrialist named Lewis Miller and a Methodist minister named John H. Vincent. In 1873 the two men decided to include instruction in secular as well as religious subjects. Authors, musicians, scientists, and politicians were invited to lecture on various topics.

The lectures were such a success that the founders of the Chautauqua Movement decided to expand the program. A four-year home-reading course called the Chautauqua Literary and Scientific Circle was offered for people who wanted to continue their studies at home. Eight thousand people joined the Circle the first year, and it continued to grow at such a rate that a monthly magazine was established to keep the members in touch with one another. The magazine, which was called *The Chautauquan,* published some of the required readings for the home-study courses along with columns of advice and encouragement from Lewis Miller and Dr. Vincent.

Most of the people who joined the Chautauqua Literary and Scientific Circle lived in rural areas of the country. They not only had no dictionaries or encyclopedias of their own, but no libraries nearby from which to borrow them. The home scholars were constantly writing in to *The Chautauquan* to ask how to pronounce or define a certain word, how to translate a French or Latin phrase, how to find out more about a particular person or place that was mentioned in one of the books.

The magazine's editor, Dr. Theodore Flood, decided that such problems could best be solved by writing explanatory notes to go with the various books and publishing them each month in *The Chautauquan*. When Dr. Flood came to Titusville and met Ida Tarbell, he asked her to take on the job.

It sounded fine to Ida. The notes would require only about two weeks of work each month. The job would give her a small income and still leave her enough time to pursue her own studies in science. Best of all, the offices of *The Chautauquan* were in Meadville. She could return to Allegheny College for graduate work.

As Ida discovered her first day on the job, Dr. Flood ran his magazine in a rather haphazard way. There were letters piled on desks and tables; a single manuscript often took hours to find. Ida, who had an instinctive sense of order, set about putting things to rights. In a few weeks the office was running so efficiently that Theodore Flood took his new employee aside.

"Miss Tarbell," he said, "I think we could use you as a permanent member of the staff."

Ida knew nothing about editing a magazine, but

the foreman of the printing shop taught her all about proofs and galleys and dummies and layouts. He showed her how to correct copy without ruining the printing plates and how to rearrange the columns when a last-minute advertisement had to be squeezed in on a page.

In addition to her duties as an editor, Ida was also expected to write some of the articles that appeared in *The Chautauquan*. One of her first pieces was an interview with the head of the United States Patent Office in Washington.

In those days the fight for woman suffrage was in full swing. The supporters of the movement had been insisting that only three hundred patents had ever been granted to women—a sure sign, they argued, that the fair sex was being stifled. The argument was supposed to arouse indignation against the patent office, but it also aroused Ida's indignation against the suffragettes. She considered it a slur on women's creative abilities. In the course of her visit to Washington she found proof that more than two thousand patents had been secured by women. Men may have denied them the vote but they had not kept them from achievements in other fields.

Ida also wrote about, and followed with great interest, a whole variety of subjects that were just beginning to absorb the nation's attention—education, slums, public health, labor unions, and the fight for an eight-hour workday.

In addition, she was very much concerned about conditions in her home state. The South Improvement Company, whose shady dealings with the railroads she remembered from her girlhood, had been absorbed by the Standard Oil Company and was trying harder than ever to monopolize the petroleum industry. Pennsylvania remained the center of the industry, and whenever Ida went back to Titusville she could see the hatred and enmity the company aroused. Ida's father was one of a small group of oil producers who managed to remain independent. They looked with scorn on the men who sold out to Standard Oil.

During July and August *The Chautauquan* suspended publication, and Ida and the rest of the staff moved out to the movement's lakefront headquarters to publish a small newspaper for the Chautauqua Assembly called *The Daily Herald*. It was a marvelous opportunity for Ida to meet some of the distinguished men who came to lecture at the Assembly.

One of them, Dr. J. P. Mahaffy, a specialist in ancient history from the University of Dublin, shared Ida's love of botany. Together they spent many hours studying the plants and flowers on the grounds at Fair Point. When Dr. Mahaffy returned to Ireland, Ida sent him some summer lily bulbs from America. In return he sent her some white poppies of a variety that had grown in Egypt at the time of the pharaohs. The poppies remained Ida's lifelong companions. They grew in her mother's garden in Titusville for years, and later in the garden of her own home in Bethel, Connecticut.

Ida earned a Master's degree from Allegheny College in 1883, but instead of going to work in a laboratory as she had always intended, she stayed on at *The Chautauquan*. Her interest in people had become stronger than her interest in things.

At that time the crusade for women's rights was constantly in the news. The suffragists were convinced that votes for women were the answer to all the problems of the world. Ida found it hard to believe. Her skepticism inspired her to make a study of women who had been active in public life in the past. She found them not much different from the men.

Among the lady politicians Ida used in her study was a woman named Madame Roland. A leader of the French Revolution, Madame Roland had later gone to her death on the guillotine. Ida was intrigued by her career. Some day, she thought, she would like to write the Frenchwoman's biography.

At first the idea was no more than a dream, but it soon began to evolve into a very definite plan. Ida had spent six years on *The Chautauquan*. The job was still interesting but it was no longer a challenge. Its main advantage was its generous salary.

Ida had decided many years before that she would never marry. In an age when women had either husbands or careers, but not both, she was too strongly committed to a career. In addition, a desire for freedom was firmly rooted in her heart. She wanted to live where she pleased, work at what she liked, and come and go at will. It was hardly the type of life that went with running a home and raising a family.

Originally Ida had turned her back on marriage because she was reluctant to lose her freedom. But now, even though she remained single, wasn't she losing her freedom anyway? If she didn't escape from *The Chautauquan* soon, she was going to be trapped there for the rest of her life.

Ida brooded about leaving the magazine for weeks, and at last she made up her mind. She was going to quit her job, move to Paris, and begin writing a biography of Madame Roland. She could support herself while she worked on it by selling free-lance articles to American newspapers and magazines.

When Ida told her friends at *The Chautauquan* of her decision, they were flabbergasted. Most of them said bluntly that she was out of her mind. She already had a good job. It would be foolish to give it up. Furthermore, she was thirty-three years old. It was too late to embark on a new career.

Dr. Flood was even more opposed to the idea. When Ida told him she was leaving to live in Paris, he stared at her in disbelief. "How will you support yourself?" he demanded.

"By writing," Ida replied.

Dr. Flood shook his head. "You're not a writer," he said. "You'll starve."

Ida's heart sank. She knew Dr. Flood was right in saying she was not a writer. She had a natural curiosity for facts and she could explain things logically, but her prose style, although clear and concise, was far from outstanding. Still, she had read enough newspaper and magazine articles to know that most of their authors were not great artists. They were simply people who became interested in something and then wrote about it in a way that made their readers interested too.

Ida went home to Titusville the following weekend to discuss her plan with her parents. Frank and Esther Tarbell obviously had misgivings about the move, but they also had confidence in their daughter's judgment.

"Frankly, Ida," her father told her, "I don't know whether it's a good idea or not. That's up to you to decide. But if you think you can do it, by all means go ahead and try."

Frank Tarbell's words were exactly what Ida had hoped to hear. "That settles it," she said firmly. "I'm on my way to France."

Chapter 5

Ida had studied French in school. She could read it well enough to translate articles from French magazines for *The Chautauquan*, but she had never had any occasion to speak it.

The only Frenchman in Titusville was a man named Monsieur Claude who ran a small cleaning and dyeing shop. One day Ida stopped in and asked the stooped, grey-haired old man if he could give her some lessons in conversational French. Monsieur Claude was flattered by her request.

"My wife and I will both converse with you," he said with a small bow. "It will be our pleasure."

When Monsieur Claude discovered that his pupil was planning to live in Paris, he sighed with envy. "My life's dream," he told her, "is to see France again before I die."

For her first lesson, Monsieur Claude made Ida learn his favorite poem, "France Adorée"—

"Beloved France." He begged her to recite it for him every time she came into the shop.

After she had withdrawn the price of her steamship ticket from her savings account, Ida had only $150 left. It would have to last until she got to Paris and could start earning money as a writer. Fortunately, two of her co-workers on *The Chautauquan* —Jo Henderson and Mary Henry—decided to join her on the trip to France.

They left in the summer of 1891. A few minutes before the boat sailed, an old friend of Mary's appeared on the dock and announced that she, too, was coming along. Ida greeted her warmly. Now there would be four of them to share the rent.

The travelers had bought a number of guidebooks to Paris. They discovered from reading them that the best place to live on a budget was on the left bank of the Seine in the section around the universities. The area was called the Latin Quarter because, in medieval times, the classes at the universities had been conducted in Latin.

The four Americans began their search for an apartment the minute they arrived in Paris. It was a discouraging task. Everything in their price range was dark and dingy. Sometimes there would be roaches or fleas skittering up the walls. Ida considered it a miracle when they finally found a pleasant and inexpensive two-bedroom flat on the Rue de Sommerard. Their landlady was a charming Frenchwoman named Madame Bonnet.

Ida had to spend part of her precious $150 for the

first month's rent. Looking at the slim roll of bills that was left in her money box, she decided to embark on her career as a writer at once. She wrote out several descriptions of her first sight of Paris and mailed them off to a number of American newspapers.

Ida could hardly believe it when one of the papers sent her a check for $5.00. She was even happier when two more checks appeared in the mail and the editors of three newspapers—the Pittsburgh *Dispatch,* the Cincinnati *Times-Star,* and the Chicago *Tribune*—wrote to say they were willing to buy her material on a regular basis.

Ida was still congratulating herself on her success when the most exciting news of all arrived. Not long after she had moved into the apartment in the Latin Quarter, Ida had written her first short story. It was about Monsieur Claude, her French teacher in Titusville. She remembered how the old man loved to hear her recite "France Adorée" and how his eyes would glow whenever he talked of his homeland. When Ida arrived in Paris, she realized at once why Monsieur Claude felt as he did. On an impulse she wrote a story about it and sent it off to *Scribner's Magazine.*

To Ida's amazement, the editor of *Scribner's,* Edward Burlingame, wrote back at once to tell her that he liked the story and wanted to publish it. A few days later, a check for $100 arrived.

The money was fabulous in itself, but *Scribner's* was also one of the most prestigious magazines in the

United States. When Ida's story appeared in it, she became something of a celebrity. Her friends back in Pennsylvania wrote to congratulate her, and several Americans who were living in Paris stopped in at Madame Bonnet's to extend their best wishes for Ida's continued success.

Although she enjoyed her brief flirtation with fame as a short-story writer, Ida was honest enough not to be deceived by her success. She knew she lacked the vivid imagination and graceful style of the true fiction writer. "France Adorée" had, after all, been only thinly disguised fact, and factual writing was the kind she did best.

Her newspaper and magazine articles described the practical everyday life of Paris—what the people ate and drank, where they lived, how they spent their Sunday afternoons. Ida was curious about these things anyway, and she was glad to have an excuse to find out more about them.

When she was not poking around Paris looking for material for her articles, Ida was invariably in one of its museums or libraries trying to learn more about Madame Roland. One day the editor of *Scribner's,* Edward Burlingame, happened to be in Paris and asked if he could call on her. Ida took advantage of his visit to ask if his publishing house would be interested in looking at the biography when it was finished. Mr. Burlingame promised to discuss it with the editors when he returned to New York. A few weeks later his reply came back: "Scribner's is looking forward to seeing your manuscript."

Despite Dr. Flood's dire prediction when she resigned from *The Chautauquan,* Ida did not starve. Not only did she write for several magazines, but a new organization called the McClure Syndicate arranged to buy her newspaper pieces and distribute them to editors around the country.

Busy as she was, Ida still found time to enjoy herself in Paris. Even something as simple as buying food became an adventure. There were a dozen small shops near the Rue de Sommerard where, for a few sous, Ida and her roommates could find the makings of an excellent dinner for four. The girls were amused to discover that housewives in Paris would buy precisely what they needed for a meal and no more. Ida sometimes came home with only an egg, two rolls, and a single cup of *café au lait.* She laughed when she recalled the tons of food her mother used to pack for family picnics on Lake Chautauqua. "The leftovers would feed a Parisian family for months," she told her friend Jo Henderson.

The girls had been living at Madame Bonnet's house for some weeks before they realized that they were the only Americans in the building. The other tenants were all Egyptians, young men from wealthy families who had come to Paris to study medicine, law, or diplomacy. On weekends and holidays they were visited by one of their countrymen, a handsome, dark-eyed cadet from the French military academy, Saint-Cyr. He was, Madame Bonnet confided to the wide-eyed Americans, a member of the Egyptian royal family, an authentic prince.

The prince and his friends were equally curious about their feminine neighbors. One Sunday afternoon they prevailed upon Madame Bonnet to knock on the girls' door and ask if they would come down and visit with the gentlemen in her salon. The girls accepted, and the visits became a weekly ritual.

Sometimes they played twenty questions or charades. Sometimes they just talked about their respective countries. Ida was impressed with the Egyptians' fluency in languages. They all spoke French, German, and English with equal ease. The Egyptians were fascinated by the independence of American women and by the strange American custom of allowing a man only one wife.

On Saturdays Ida and her roommates went sightseeing. They made it a rule to go someplace different every week. Sometimes it was a ride on the *bateaux-mouches,* the colorful sightseeing boats that plied up and down the Seine; sometimes, a visit to Louis XIV's splendid palace at Versailles. Occasionally they took longer excursions to see the cathedrals at Chartres and Rheims or to visit the *châteaux* in Beauvais and Compiègne.

Ida planned to remain in Paris until she finished her biography of Madame Roland, but her roommates were going home at the end of the summer.

"Before we leave," Jo Henderson suggested, "let's all take a farewell vacation."

The girls talked it over and finally decided to visit the rocky island of Mont Saint-Michel off the northwest coast of France.

A few days before they were to leave, Ida had a surprise visit from Samuel S. McClure, the owner of the newspaper syndicate she wrote for in the United States.

S. S. McClure, as he usually signed himself, dashed up the four flights of stairs and charged into Ida's sitting room flourishing a heavy gold pocket watch.

"I only have ten minutes to talk to you," he announced breathlessly. "I have to catch a train for Geneva."

It was the first time Ida had met the syndicate owner. He was close to her own age, a slight man with lively blue eyes, an unruly shock of sandy hair, and a habit of taking over conversations. Ida knew she should be asking him questions about the kind of articles he would like to buy from her and the price he would be willing to pay for them. Instead she sat spellbound while McClure told her his life history—how he had worked his way through Knox College in Illinois, his courtship of his wife Hattie, how he had founded his newspaper syndicate, his plans to launch a new magazine.

Ida was particularly excited by McClure's idea for a magazine. At that point in its history, the nation had only four important magazines: *Harper's, Scribner's, The Century,* and *The Atlantic Monthly.* They all cost twenty-five cents or more and they appealed almost exclusively to the upper classes.

McClure wanted this magazine to be completely different. He hoped to sell it for fifteen cents, and he wanted to edit it not just for people who were wealthy and well educated but for ordinary readers —shopgirls and laborers, housewives and clerks.

Ida became as enthusiastic as her visitor at the prospect. Before she had a chance to say so, S. S. McClure suddenly looked down at the gold watch in his hand. The ten-minute visit had stretched into two hours. "Good heavens!" McClure cried, abruptly leaping to his feet. "I must go. Can you lend me forty dollars?"

By coincidence, Ida had taken $40.00 from her bank account that very morning to finance her vacation at Mont Saint-Michel. The money was sitting in an envelope on her desk. She picked it up and handed it to S. S. McClure.

He took the envelope with a quick thank-you, and as he reached for the doorknob, remarked, "How odd that you should have that much money in the house."

"Isn't it?" Ida said, without mentioning her vacation. "It's never happened before."

McClure had no sooner disappeared down the long staircase than Ida began to regret giving away her hard-earned money. She liked McClure, but he was obviously a disorganized man. He would probably forget about the loan the minute he walked out the door.

"I'll have to give up my vacation," Ida thought grimly. Then she sighed. "It serves me right for being such a ninny."

Ida was wrong about S. S. McClure. He wired his London office to send her a check, and the $40.00

arrived in plenty of time to pay for the trip to Mont Saint-Michel.

Ida's first year in Paris had seemed full of adventure. Her second was more routine. She still loved the city but she was beginning to miss her family. Every letter with a United States postmark was eagerly ripped open and its contents read not once, but several times over. Ida loved to hear every tiny detail of what was happening back in Titusville— what was playing at the Opera House, who came for dinner and what they ate, how the poppies in her garden had survived the summer.

One Sunday morning Ida woke up feeling strangely down in the dumps. She could not help thinking that something must be wrong at home. Too depressed to work, she finally picked up the Sunday paper, *Le Temps.* As usual, she turned first to the news from the United States. There she read with horror that Titusville and its neighbor, Oil City, had been totally destroyed by a flash fire and flood. According to the newspaper, everyone in the two cities had either drowned or been burned to death.

Distraught, Ida rushed out to the nearest kiosk and snatched up every paper on the stand. Some were in French, some in English. All carried the same tragic story. Ida spent a miserable night. She was haunted by visions of her family dead, their home in ruins. The next morning Madame Bonnet knocked on her door with a cablegram. Ida unfolded it with trembling fingers. It was from her brother Will and there was just one word: SAFE.

A letter arrived at the end of the week with the news that the towns had indeed been badly damaged but that the Tarbells had all survived the disaster. Ida breathed a quick prayer of thanksgiving and vowed to finish her book and return to Titusville as quickly as possible.

Chapter 6

In 1893 Samuel McClure started the new magazine he had talked about during his whirlwind visit to Ida's Paris flat. It was called *McClure's Magazine*, and Ida became a regular contributor. Her first assignment was a series of articles on the achievements of the great French and English scientists.

Ida loved it. At last she had a chance to use the scientific knowledge she had worked so hard to acquire at Allegheny. Equally exciting, it was a chance to meet some of the most prominent scientists of the century, including the renowned Louis Pasteur.

Ida interviewed the famous bacteriologist in his apartment at the scientific institute he had founded. She found him relaxed and perfectly willing to talk to her about his life and work. When Ida asked if she might have some informal pictures to illustrate her story, Madame Pasteur obligingly took out their family photo album, and the three of them spent the afternoon poring over its contents.

When it was time for their guest to leave, Louis Pasteur and his wife escorted her to the door. As Ida made her way down the dimly lit stairs, the great man kept calling after her, "Be careful, don't trip in the dark."

In theory, Ida had enough assignments to support herself. In reality, she was desperate for money.

A few weeks after the first issue of *McClure's* appeared, the United States was hit by the panic of 1893. Banks failed, businesses went bankrupt, and thousands of people were thrown out of work.

The panic lasted from April to October. Samuel McClure, caught in the middle of it, could find neither advertisers nor readers for his new magazine. His debts grew so large that for a while he never read the evening paper without first turning to the list of people who had gone bankrupt. He was always sure he was going to find his name among them.

Samuel McClure borrowed money, wangled credit, and fought off bill collectors—and somehow *McClure's* stayed alive. But the new magazine was so heavily in debt that it was going to be several months before he could afford to pay his writers.

Ida, in Paris, received the news calmly. She had been following America's financial problems in the newspapers and she had already steeled herself for the worst. There was no point in getting upset, she decided. It was more important to try and figure out a way to survive.

It was July. Ida knew it would be a long time be-

55

fore she had any use for the sealskin coat that was hanging in the back of her clothes closet. She had bought it when she was working on *The Chautauquan,* and it was by far the most extravagant item in her wardrobe. Ida took out the coat and ran her hand gently across the sleek black fur. Then she resolutely folded it over her arm and marched out to find the nearest pawnshop.

She found one only a few blocks from where she lived. It was crammed with an assortment of possessions—a silver teapot, a black silk opera hat, sapphire cuff links, and dozens of gold watches that other impoverished Parisians had left as collateral for loans.

When Ida stepped up to the pawnbroker's window and showed him the sealskin coat, the man eyed her warily. She was a stranger, and a foreigner besides. He shrugged. "How do I know you didn't steal it?" he demanded.

Ida was torn between anger and amusement at the suggestion. She could feel her face flush but she gave him her name and address and explained that she was an American journalist. The man continued to stare at her skeptically. "Can you show me something to prove that you are who you say you are?" he said at last.

"Just wait," Ida told him. "I'll be back in a few minutes."

Leaving the coat on the counter she raced back to her flat and started rummaging through her desk. She had no idea what kind of proof the man needed, but she took anything that she thought might help —a handful of letters, an old checkbook, and, on an impulse, her Allegheny College diploma. She returned to the pawnshop a few minutes later and dumped them on the counter beside the fur coat. "Will these do?" she asked breathlessly.

The pawnbroker peered at the haphazard assortment of identification papers as if he suspected that they, too, had been stolen. He looked through the letters and the checkbook, shook his head, and thrust them back at her with a scowl.

Ida's heart sank. The sealskin coat was her only hope. If she couldn't get a loan on it, she had no idea where she would find the money to support herself. She watched anxiously as the pawnbroker picked up the last item, the heavy parchment diploma she had earned at Allegheny. He studied the Latin inscription, and was obviously very much impressed. Ida didn't see how it proved that she was Ida Tarbell any more than the other papers she had brought along, but she kept her thoughts to herself.

To her immense relief the man finished appraising the diploma, took the fur coat, and counted out enough francs to pay her expenses until *McClure's* could afford to send her a check for her work. A college degree certainly comes in handy, Ida thought, as she walked out of the pawnshop with the money in her purse.

Ida finished her biography of Madame Roland in the summer of 1894. The manuscript needed only minor revisions, and these could be done just as easily in Titusville as in Paris. She sailed home in June, anxious to see her family but just as anxious to return to Paris as quickly as possible.

The old house in Titusville was unchanged, but Frank and Esther Tarbell seemed much older. They had lost most of their savings during the previous year's depression. Ida noticed how her mother turned down the gas lamps when they weren't being used and how carefully she mended every stitch of clothing to make it last a little bit longer.

Ida's father had worked hard all his life; she was sorry he couldn't enjoy a more carefree old age. But Frank and Esther Tarbell seemed unperturbed by their financial reverses. They were content to enjoy their home and family and their work for the Methodist church. Ida's brother Will was married now, and he and his wife, Ella, lived only a few doors down the street. Will's children, two girls and a boy, were a great source of joy to their grandparents. For the first time in years, Frank Tarbell had an excuse to go to the circus when it came to town, and Esther could pack her lunch baskets for a new generation of famished picnickers.

S. S. McClure had asked Ida to join the staff of *McClure's Magazine* when she returned to the United States. Ida had agreed, but first she needed time to make the final revisions on her book. She had barely finished when she received a frantic letter from McClure. He wanted her to come to New York at once and write a life of Napoleon Bonaparte.

When she arrived in S. S. McClure's office a few

days later, Ida discovered the reason for the rush. Some months earlier a wealthy Washingtonian named Gardiner Green Hubbard had given McClure permission to publish his valuable collection of pictures of Napoleon. The only proviso was that Hubbard would have the right to approve whatever text the magazine used to accompany the pictures. McClure agreed, found a writer, and with great fanfare announced that the first installment of the Napoleon series would appear in the *McClure's* November issue.

Gardiner Hubbard was an admirer of Napoleon. McClure's writer, an Englishman, detested him. Hubbard took one look at the story he sent in and pronounced it dreadful. By then it was August. If the biography was to appear on schedule in November, it would have to be ready in less than two months.

"Two months," Ida groaned. "I've just spent two years writing a biography of Madame Roland, and she wasn't half as important as Napoleon!"

S. S. McClure gave her one of his most engaging smiles. "You can do it," he said confidently.

Ida secretly hoped that her new assignment would necessitate another visit to Paris, but as it turned out, all the research material she needed was in Washington, D. C. The State Department, the Library of Congress, and Gardiner Hubbard himself all had excellent reference books and documents about Napoleon.

Mr. Hubbard and his wife lived at Twin Oaks, a

spacious estate just outside of Washington. Ida was dazzled by the big house with its fine furnishings and well-tended gardens. She felt out of place amidst such opulent surroundings, but the Hubbards seemed not to notice her plain clothes and small-town background. They treated her as graciously as they treated their more sophisticated and socially prominent friends.

Ida quickly lost her self-consciousness. She only felt ill at ease when Samuel McClure appeared at Twin Oaks. McClure would come to Washington without notice and burst into the Hubbards' drawing room. He usually had a satchelful of page proofs in his hand. These tentative layouts for the Napoleon story would be spread out on the elegant carpets while McClure discoursed for hours about how fabulous it was going to be.

Ida was so embarrassed by his rude behavior that she felt she ought to apologize for him. Mrs. Hubbard assured her that no apology was necessary. "That eagerness of his is beautiful," she said. "Please don't worry. I'm accustomed to geniuses."

In order to meet her deadline for the Napoleon biography, Ida put herself on a strict schedule. She started working by eight thirty each morning and often stayed at her desk until ten or eleven o'clock at night. For the first two weeks she did nothing but research, reading everything she could find about the French emperor, from his birth on Corsica to his death in exile on the island of St. Helena.

After that she was ready to begin writing. She worked a six-day week, allowing herself a day off on Sunday, not only out of respect for the Sabbath but also because she needed a day to relax and unwind.

By ignoring everything else and concentrating solely on her work, Ida was able to finish a first draft of the Napoleon book in a little more than a month. It took another few days of rewriting, rechecking, and retyping before the manuscript was ready for submission.

Thanks to the grueling pace she set for herself, Ida managed to finish the biography in a record six weeks. To her astonishment, Mr. Hubbard pronounced it a first-rate job, and Samuel McClure, with a flood of congratulations to the exhausted author, rushed it off to the printers.

Ida was even more amazed when the biography was published in *McClure's*. Several distinguished scholars wrote to commend her on the work, and Charles Bonaparte, the grandson of Napoleon's youngest brother, Jérôme, invited her to lunch at his home in Baltimore and showed her some of his own mementos of his famous relative.

After its serialization in *McClure's* the Napoleon biography was published as a book. It was the second book Ida had written, and it proved helpful in getting her first one into print. She had sent the Madame Roland manuscript to Scribner's but the editors had been hemming and hawing about it for weeks. When her life of Napoleon was received so enthusiastically, they finally decided that Ida had enough talent to be added to their list of authors. Ironically, after the two years she had spent on Madame Roland, the book never sold as well as the shorter biography of Napoleon that she had written in a mere six weeks.

Chapter 7

When Ida originally joined the staff of *McClure's* she thought of it as a temporary job. As soon as she finished her assignment on Napoleon, she would return to Paris, resume her career as a free-lance journalist, and specialize in writing books about French history. By the time the biography was completed, however, she changed her mind. She liked the security of a weekly paycheck and she was enjoying her co-workers on the magazine.

She was stimulated by S. S. McClure's enthusiasm; she also admired his calmer partner, the magazine's co-editor, John S. Phillips. A brilliant man and a fine editor, Phillips had a talent for coaxing writers into doing their best work for him. Ida liked the magazine McClure and Phillips had created. It was young and lively and always tried to have what its owners called a "lift."

Other publishers often sneered at *McClure's* and called it cheap. It was, but only as far as its price was concerned. Its quality was hard to match. The list of fiction writers who appeared in it was a who's who of literature. There were Robert Louis Stevenson, Rudyard Kipling, Arthur Conan Doyle, H. G. Wells, Stephen Crane, and Willa Cather.

On the nonfiction side, S. S. McClure had very definite ideas about the kinds of things the magazine should publish. He wanted to deal with subjects that would interest a wide variety of readers and to treat them in a factual, yet lively, style. When he read the articles Ida sent back to the United States from France, he became obsessed with the idea of hiring her to write for *McClure's*.

His partner, John Phillips, tried to convince him that they needed someone who was better known and more experienced. He also hinted that a man might be easier to work with than a woman. McClure, who took great delight in defying his critics, brushed aside Phillips' objections and hired Ida anyway. She turned out to be the salvation of *McClure's*.

At that point, the magazine had been in business for over a year and had yet to make a profit. Then, in November 1894, Ida's life of Napoleon appeared. The magazine's circulation rose from 35,000 to 65,000 copies. S. S. McClure was overjoyed. For the first time in the year and a half since it had started, it was beginning to look as if his magazine might survive.

Samuel McClure promptly decided that Ida ought to follow up the Napoleon triumph with a series on Abraham Lincoln. His staff greeted the idea with dismay. Nobody wanted to read about Lincoln, they told him. Moreover, a rival publication, *The Century Magazine,* had already published a long excerpt from a ten-volume biography by two of Lincoln's private secretaries, John Nicolay and John Hay. There was no point in trying to compete with that.

McClure ignored the staff's objections. In his opinion Lincoln was the greatest man in history. He couldn't believe the American public didn't want to read anything and everything about him. As for *The Century,* he was too confident of his own editorial hunches to worry about what they had done.

"They tell me that only my inexperience as a magazine editor leads me to compete with *The Century,*" he told John Phillips wryly. "Well, inexperience is a thing that doesn't last. Maybe I'd better use it while I still have it."

Ida had her own reasons for being unenthusiastic about S. S. McClure's new proposal. She considered herself a specialist in French, not American, history, and her initial impulse was to turn the assignment down. Then she thought it over and decided that perhaps she was taking herself too seriously.

She did share McClure's admiration for Lincoln. Although she was too young to remember the slain president, her parents had spoken of him with a respect close to reverence. It was almost thirty years ago, but Ida could still recall the sorrowful droop of her father's shoulders when he trudged up the hill to their home in Rouseville with the news of the tragedy at Ford's Theater.

Ida agreed to write the biography of Abraham Lincoln, but she began to regret the decision the instant she found out what S. S. McClure had in mind.

He was convinced that there were dozens of unpublished pictures and reminiscences of Abraham Lincoln. Ida didn't see how there could be. Lincoln's law partner, William Herndon, had already collected his speeches and correspondence and used them in a biography. Whatever he had missed was sure to be in the ten volumes by Nicolay and Hay.

"What more can I dig up?" Ida said dolefully.

McClure ignored her pessimism. "Out with you," he ordered. "Look, see. Report. You'll find plenty if you'll only try."

Ida left for Kentucky and the first step in her research mission on a bitter cold day in February 1895. Samuel McClure was on hand to see her off. No longer the imperious editor, he suddenly became quite solicitous for her comfort. "Have you warm bedsocks?" he inquired anxiously as he escorted her to the train. "If not, we'll send you some. It will be awful in those Kentucky hotels."

As Samuel McClure had feared, it was indeed cold in Kentucky's hotels. Worse yet, Ida's quest for Lincoln memorabilia appeared to be in vain. Weeks of searching in the region where he had spent his early years turned up nothing more than an unimportant letter, a few old newspaper clippings, and some court records in which the Lincoln family name appeared.

The discouraged researcher finally had a stroke of good fortune when the news of her undertaking reached her friend Emily Lyons. Ida had met Mrs. Lyons at the Hubbards' estate in Washington. She lived in Chicago and seemed to know everyone in the country who was worth knowing.

As soon as she heard that Ida was hunting for mementos of Abraham Lincoln, Emily Lyons invited her to come to Chicago. "I'll see that you meet Robert Lincoln," she promised, "and I'll see that he gives you something."

The day after Ida stepped off the train from New York, she found herself in Mrs. Lyons' drawing room having tea with Abraham Lincoln's son, Robert. Her hostess lost no time in getting to the point. "Now Robert," she said, "I want you to give her something worthwhile."

Still dazed at finding herself face to face with the president's son, Ida could hardly believe her luck when Robert Lincoln laughed good naturedly and said, "Of course, I'll give her something if you say so, Emily."

Lincoln told Ida that most of his father's papers had already been taken by his other biographers. "But I have one thing that might interest you," he said. "An early portrait of my father that has never been published."

The picture was a priceless acquisition. It showed

a gentle, thoughtful Lincoln, his face still unscarred by the burdens of his presidency. Samuel McClure made copies of the photo and sent them to various prominent people for comments. Woodrow Wilson, who was just gaining fame as an orator and political thinker, called it a notable picture and remarked on "the expression of the dreaminess, the familiar face without its sadness." Charles Dudley Warner, a well-known writer of the day, said it was far and away the most outstanding presentation of Lincoln that he had ever seen. Both the portrait and the comments were used to introduce the *McClure's* series on Abraham Lincoln. They caused exactly the sensation S. S. McClure had hoped for.

Once the first installment of the biography was published, Ida's search for Lincoln documents became more fruitful. Readers of *McClure's* began looking in their attics, and a number of them discovered letters and speeches that had been gathering dust for decades. Several forgotten pictures also came to light. Robert Lincoln was so thrilled at the way Ida's book was being received that he promised to see her anytime she wished and to help her in any way he could with her research.

Ida spent more than two years working on her biography of Lincoln. She traveled up and down the state of Illinois, trying to get a feeling for the places where Lincoln had lived and worked. She found people who had known him, and she quizzed them intensively about the way he had looked and talked and the kind of stories he had told.

Occasionally she turned up evidence that some of the things already printed about Lincoln were untrue. William Herndon, for instance, told in his book how Lincoln had supposedly neglected to show up for his first wedding to his wife, Mary Todd. Ida checked the story with several of Mrs. Lincoln's relatives and found that no such wedding had ever been arranged. In fact, one of Mrs. Lincoln's sisters pointed out that Herndon had also let his imagination roam to the extent of dressing the disappointed bride in a white silk dress. "Impossible," the woman scoffed. "Mary Lincoln never had a white silk dress until she went to Washington."

Ida talked to a number of people who had heard the Lincoln-Douglas debates. Their eyewitness descriptions were invaluable, but she was even more intrigued by their constant references to another of Lincoln's speeches. Time and again, someone she was interviewing in reference to the debates with Stephan Douglas would remark, "Well, those were good speeches, but they were nothing like the Lost Speech. That was the greatest thing Lincoln ever did."

The Lost Speech, Ida discovered, had been given at the Republican State Convention of 1856. The reporters who covered the convention had been so stirred by the speech that they had completely forgotten to take notes. In fact, by the time Lincoln finished talking, they were all standing on top of their desks to get a closer look at the gifted orator. When Ida tracked down some of the journalists who had been at the convention, they corroborated everything she had already learned.

Still she was not satisfied. There had to be a record of the speech somewhere—perhaps not a word-by-word transcription, but at least a few notes to capture the gist of it. Ida continued the search until finally she came across the name of Henry C. Whitney. Whitney had been a circuit lawyer with Lincoln but now practiced law in Massachusetts. Ida went up to see him.

Whitney received her politely. Yes, he had heard the famous speech, he told her. In fact, he still had a few notes on it he had taken. They were so sketchy that at first the aging lawyer was reluctant to show them to his visitor. It took all of Ida's persuasive powers to talk him into it.

Still not daring to get her hopes up, Ida studied the carefully preserved scraps of yellowing paper. They seemed authentic, but she always checked her facts carefully before putting them into print. She borrowed the notes and showed them to some of the people who had first mentioned the Lost Speech to her. One or two of them still refused to believe that any record of the legendary speech existed, but the rest agreed that Whitney had captured the tone, the arguments, and even many of the phrases that Lincoln had used.

Ida was further encouraged when she showed the notes to Joseph Medill. Now editor of the Chicago *Tribune,* Medill had been at the state convention of 1856 and was one of the reporters who had climbed on top of his desk and forgotten to write anything down. Medill took a look at Henry Whitney's notes and pronounced them a reasonably accurate reproduction of Lincoln's Lost Speech. On the strength of his judgment, *McClure's* published the notes along with the story of how Ida Tarbell had managed to track them down.

The Abraham Lincoln biography proved, without a doubt, that Samuel McClure was a genius at judging the public's taste in reading. The mere announcement that the biography would appear started a rise in the magazine's sales. When the first installment was published in November 1895, 190,-000 copies were sold; when the second installment came out, the circulation climbed to more than 250,000. There was no problem finding advertisers now. Companies by the dozen wanted to boast about their wares in a magazine that was being bought and read so widely. Samuel McClure was soon known as the most successful publisher in the business. *McClure's* became the leading magazine, and Ida Tarbell the nation's foremost woman writer.

Chapter 8

After its original success as a magazine series, Ida's life of Abraham Lincoln was published as a book. Her research involved her in two subsequent books. The first was Charles A. Dana's *Recollections of the Civil War*.

Dana, who was then in his seventies, was the editor of the New York *Sun*. Thirty years before he had served as Lincoln's assistant secretary of war; his job was to bring back eyewitness accounts of the fighting to the president.

The newspaper editor was obviously a valuable source of information on Lincoln's conduct of the war, but Ida was afraid to approach him. She had never met Charles Dana; she knew him only through his brilliant but biting editorials in the *Sun*. Ida suspected that he was as sharp-tongued in person as he was in print, and she had no desire to tangle with him.

When she said as much at the office one day, John

Phillips and Samuel McClure, who both knew Dana, rebuked her for her fears. "There's no need to feel that way," Phillips assured her. "Mr. Dana is a gentleman."

McClure agreed. Always the more aggressive of the two partners, he added, "I'll take care of it for you."

Samuel McClure went to see Charles Dana and not only arranged for Ida to talk to him about Lincoln but also extracted a promise from Dana to tell the story of his war experiences for *McClure's*. Ida would do the writing and work out a plan for conducting the interviews.

Ida was still leery of confronting Charles Dana but she knew that she had to go through with it. First, however, she needed to do some research on her own so that she could discuss the Civil War intelligently with him. She began by studying the official government records, which were then in the process of being edited.

Leslie Perry, the lean, stern-faced man who was in charge of the Civil War archives, was not very happy about giving Ida access to them. Mr. Perry was convinced that women had no business poking their noses into history, especially the history of a war. "How can you possibly understand it?" he demanded when Ida went to see him.

Since the records were government property, Mr. Perry had to make them available to her, but he beamed with delight every time he caught her describing a battle inaccurately. "That's what comes from allowing a woman to write history," he would chortle triumphantly.

Despite his disdain for her efforts, Leslie Perry proved to be a great help in ferreting out Charles Dana's official reports and dispatches. Ida studied them thoroughly before making an appointment for her first interview with the *Sun*'s editor.

They met in his office, and Ida found Dana as formidable as she had expected. Worse yet, he was already beginning to regret promising his Civil War memoirs to *McClure's*. "I'm not interested in what I did in the past," he growled. "I'm only interested in the present. I'm trying to keep up with the world of today. I'm studying Russian now—a very fascinating language. I don't want to bother with what I did in the Civil War. What do you propose?"

Ida outlined her plan as briefly as she could. She wanted to see Dana three afternoons a week. She would prepare a set of questions in advance and a stenographer from *McClure's* would come with her to take down his answers. Dana agreed, and Ida spent most of the winter of 1896 and '97 listening to his recollections of the war years.

It was a fascinating slice of history. Dana had seen some of the most important battles of the war and had known many of the Union generals, including Ulysses S. Grant. The editor was an old man but he had a remarkably keen memory. It enabled Ida to fill in the details of the reports she had already unearthed during her preliminary research with Leslie Perry.

Ida rarely completed an assignment without making new friends. The Napoleon book introduced her to Mr. and Mrs. Gardiner Hubbard, and the Lincoln book to Robert Lincoln, but with Charles Dana her relationship was strictly business. They never talked about anything but the Civil War.

Dana's *Recollections* were published in *McClure's,* and later as a book, under his own name. Naturally, they had to be written as if Dana himself was speaking. Ida, still intimidated by the editor, was understandably fearful about showing him the completed manuscript.

It was finished in the summer of 1897, and the serialization was to begin in the November issue. Charles Dana had gone to London for the summer, and Ida, with great trepidation, sent the page proofs over for his approval. To her immense relief, they came back with only minor corrections and no further comment. Ida hoped Charles Dana liked the book she had ghostwritten for him but she never had a chance to find out. Mr. Dana died a few weeks before the first installment appeared in *McClure's.*

The second book to evolve from Ida's research into the life of Abraham Lincoln was Carl Schurz's *Reminiscences.* Schurz, a German immigrant, had had a varied career as diplomat, soldier, newspaperman, and politician. He had assisted Lincoln in his senate race against Stephen Douglas and in his 1860 campaign for the presidency. He had also played a leading role, till then unpublicized, in helping the president formulate the Emancipation Proclamation.

Ida saw at once that Schurz's story would make an

excellent magazine series and begged him to write it for *McClure's.* Having already refused an offer from Richard Watson Gilder, the editor of *The Century,* Schurz didn't see how he would be able to sell the story to anyone else. Ida persisted, and gradually Schurz began to weaken. His long years of government service had given him no chance to amass any money, and he was concerned about providing for his family after his death. When S. S. McClure offered him a generous price for his work, he finally gave in.

Carl Schurz wrote the book on his own; Ida's job was to edit the manuscript, suggesting ways to reorganize or reword certain sections and urging him to extend or embellish some of the incidents.

Ida made several visits to Schurz's summer home in upper New York State. The house stood in the woods overlooking Lake George. Ida liked the fresh smell of the pine trees and the clean mountain air but she was most enchanted by Schurz himself. Like Charles Dana, he was in his seventies, but unlike Dana, he was as cheerful and exuberant as a college boy. He loved music, and Ida enjoyed listening to him singing selections from Wagner's operas as he was getting ready for breakfast in the morning. Sometimes he would stop working abruptly and get up and play a few selections on the piano before returning to his desk. Ida was sorry when the series was finished and she had no further excuse to visit the delightful old man.

Although she was often on the road in pursuit of

stories, or in New York for editorial conferences at *McClure's,* Ida spent most of her time in Washington, D.C. She remained friends with Gardiner Hubbard and his wife, and through them became acquainted with many leading diplomats and statesmen as well as a number of well-known scientists.

The Hubbards' daughter, Mabel, was married to Alexander Graham Bell. Ida had a chance to meet the handsome inventor along with some of his equally clever friends. One, Dr. Samuel Pierpont Langley, the astronomer and physicist who was director of the Smithsonian Institution, had been trying to develop a machine that would fly. Many people considered him insane, but in 1896 Langley actually succeeded in building an "air runner" that stayed aloft over the Potomac River.

Ida did not witness the flight, but Alexander Graham Bell described it for her. The air runner was launched from a houseboat anchored in the river. It soared more than a hundred feet above the water, flew in a wide circle above the treetops along the shore, and then returned to land serenely on the river. Although the machine's flight was agonizingly brief, S. S. McClure sensed its possibilities and sent Ida to interview Dr. Langley.

She asked him to tell her all about this flying machine so she could write about it for *McClure's.* "But no scientific jargon, please," she begged with a smile. "We want it in language so simple that I can understand it, because if I can understand it, all the world can."

Ida's interviews with Samuel Langley won her another friend. When the article was finished, he was so pleased with it that he gave her a special treat—a trip to the Washington zoo with the zoo's director in tow to make sure that the kangaroo jumped and the hyena laughed for her.

Ida, S. S. McClure, and John Phillips were tremendously excited about the early experiments with flight, but the article in *McClure's* was greeted with scorn by more than a few readers. Ida couldn't help being reminded of Professor Jeremiah Tingley's lecture on the telephone that had caused some of her fellow students at Allegheny to sneer at him as a dreamer.

One of Ida's favorite friends in Washington was the Republican senator from Massachusetts, George Frisbie Hoar. Now in his seventies, the genial politician was one of the oldest members of Congress. Ida had met the senator and his wife through Mr. and Mrs. Hubbard. She had been captivated by Hoar's fund of witty stories and by the way he could recite so beautifully from the Greek and Roman poets, but she was even more impressed with his unflagging determination to improve his country.

Senator Hoar had been one of the few politicians in the nation to denounce the militantly anti-Catholic American Protective Association. He had sponsored several bills to curb the lobbyists who swarmed into Washington and specialized in persuading congressmen to vote in favor of the interests they represented. He had also been a leader in demanding punishment for officials found guilty of dishonesty in the government's dealings with the Indians.

Not content with fighting for decency and justice, the senator was also concerned with developing the intellectual aspects of American life. He had been one of the leaders in organizing the Library of Congress and the Smithsonian Institution. In his hometown of Worcester, Massachusetts, he had helped found Clark University and the Worcester Polytechnic Institute.

Ida's life of Abraham Lincoln had taken her away from France and immersed her in the history of the United States. Her friendship with Senator Hoar inspired her to take an even greater interest in the land of her birth. She had already achieved fame as a writer. The royalties she was accumulating from her books were rapidly making her rich as well. But money as such had little interest for Ida. Most of her earnings were sent back to Titusville to help make her parents more comfortable in their old age.

At forty, Ida's ambition was much the same as it had been at twenty—to do something worthwhile with her life. She had already flirted with careers in science and teaching; she had experimented with writing French history. Now, for the first time in many years, she began to take a closer look at her own country.

She believed deeply in America but she knew that it was a far from perfect society. There was corruption in politics and injustice in business; prejudice and poverty were commonplace, and, most tragic of all, only a handful of people seemed to care. As a writer, Ida was not sure how much she could do to bring the nation's problems to the attention of her countrymen, but she felt she had an obligation to try.

Chapter 9

Ida's decision came at a time when *McClure's,* too, was changing its focus. The magazine had scored its original success by featuring articles about famous people. During the Spanish-American War, however, it began to concentrate on current events. After the war the editors decided to continue this policy. They were less interested in the news as such, and more concerned with exploring the social problems of the day.

By now S. S. McClure had added two more journalist-editors to his staff. One was Lincoln Steffens, who would soon become famous for his exposé of municipal corruption, *The Shame of the Cities.* The other was Ray Stannard Baker, who would write an impressive biography of Woodrow Wilson and—under his pen name, David Grayson—a series of delightful essays about rural life in the United States.

In addition, the magazine was still publishing

some of the best fiction of the day—stories by Booth Tarkington, Jack London, and a young man named W. S. Porter, who would later sign himself O. Henry. McClure also acquired the American rights to two of Joseph Conrad's most famous novels, *Heart of Darkness* and *Lord Jim,* and to Bram Stoker's memorable tale of terror, *Dracula.*

Ida had left Washington and now lived in a small apartment in New York. She did some of her writing at home; more often she worked at her desk in the *McClure's* offices on Lexington Avenue between Twenty-fifth and Twenty-sixth streets.

At lunchtime Ida, Lincoln Steffens, Ray Stannard Baker, and John Phillips usually strolled across the street to the Ashland House. They ate in the small private dining room at the rear of the restaurant and sometimes they were joined by a distinguished guest. Once it was Admiral Robert Peary, the Arctic explorer; another day, Guglielmo Marconi, the inventor of the wireless telegraph.

Few of the guests were surprised to find a woman at the lunch table. Journalism was more advanced than the other professions, and an occasional feminine byline appeared in the newspapers and magazines. Of the half dozen or so women who worked in the field, however, none was as highly regarded as Ida Tarbell.

In the early days of *McClure's* someone once asked Richard Watson Gilder, the editor of *The Century Magazine,* what he thought of his new rival. Gilder dismissed it with a sneer. "They got a girl to write a life of Lincoln," he remarked by way of explanation.

But Gilder soon discovered what S. S. McClure had known all along. Ida Tarbell was not just a "girl"; she was a first-rate journalist.

The other members of the *McClure's* staff respected Ida's talents as a writer and editor, but they also found her an intelligent, good-humored companion and a trusted friend. Since she signed her articles Ida M. Tarbell, they affectionately nicknamed her Idarem.

Lincoln Steffens wrote in his autobiography:

She knew each one of us and all our idiosyncracies and troubles. She had none of her own so far as we ever heard. When we were deadlocked we might each of us send for her and down she would come to the office, smiling like a tall good looking young mother to say "Hush children." She would pick out the sense in each of our contentions and putting them together with her own good sense, give me a victory over S. S., him a triumph over Phillips and take away from all of us only the privilege of gloating. The interest of the magazine was pointed out and we and she went back to work.

The *McClure's* staff had a special devotion to their magazine. In the few short years since its inception it had become the most widely read publication in the country. Much of its popularity was due to S. S. McClure's insistence on publishing lively, timely material, but several other factors also contributed to its success.

The 1890's brought about some revolutionary changes in the magazine business. New developments in photoengraving lowered the cost of reproducing illustrations. A new type of glazed paper also became available, replacing the more expensive rag paper that had been used before. As the cost of publishing went down, the opportunities for selling a magazine went up.

In the years between 1880 and 1900 the population of the United States doubled. Moreover, the new public high schools had created an intelligent reading public, ready and eager to buy a magazine that appealed to their interests.

Advertisers were as important to the magazines as subscribers, and here, too, things had never been better. With the increase in the country's population, new businesses were started and old ones expanded. The competition for customers became so keen that manufacturers began to make up clever slogans and buy ads in newspapers and magazines to persuade the public that their products were better than anyone else's.

The years between 1890 and 1918 have been called the Golden Age of the American magazine. For fifteen of those years—1895 to 1910—*McClure's* reigned supreme. Everyone on the staff basked in the glory of its success.

Ida liked the feeling of vitality she got from the magazine; she had the freedom to explore new ideas and the opportunity to meet new people. Above all, she welcomed the chance to combine her social conscience with her career. *McClure's* dealt with most of the major problems that confronted the country, and Ida helped determine its stand on all of them.

S. S. McClure had several pet subjects. One was the dishonesty of big-city politicians; another was the constant wrangling between labor and management; still another was trusts.

The rapid growth of big business in the United States had led to many abuses. In more than one instance large companies had joined forces to seize control of a particular industry by forming a trust. Small independent owners in the field were then driven out of business and the trust was left with a monopoly. It could pay whatever wages and charge whatever prices it wanted. Neither workers nor customers had any place else to go.

S. S. McClure had been thinking about publishing a series of articles on trusts for a long time. The best way to go about it, he had decided, was to concentrate on a particular industry and trace its history, showing how and why the trust was formed and how it affected both the industry and the people involved in it.

McClure knew that Ida Tarbell was the best writer for the job. She would have no qualms about taking on the enormous amount of work it would entail. When McClure called her into his office to discuss the series, Ida agreed that concentrating on one trust was the best idea. She suggested the one recently formed by John Pierpont Morgan, the United States Steel Corporation.

Ida started collecting material on the steel trust, but after several weeks of work her enthusiasm began to wane. Somehow the subject didn't seem quite right. She might have dropped the idea completely, but McClure kept after her. If steel was no good, why didn't she try another industry?

A *McClure's* reader had written to suggest a piece about the sugar trust, which was not only able to control the price of sugar but also had enough power in Congress to influence the tariffs on it. Ida considered the suggestion for a while, but she knew sugar wasn't right either. It would have to be something bigger and more important.

The suggestion was put in the files along with the unfinished research on steel. The series on trusts was on the verge of being put off indefinitely when a letter from Ray Stannard Baker arrived. McClure liked to send his editors roaming about the country in search of ideas. Baker, who was on the West Coast, thought he had the makings of a good article on the discovery of oil in California.

Oil? McClure shook his head. The idea didn't appeal to him at all. Ida was equally cool to it. Not until weeks later did it occur to her that Baker's letter contained the answer to the series on trusts.

The Standard Oil Company was the first and, for many years, the largest of the trusts. It owned almost forty thousand miles of pipelines and manufactured more than 86 percent of the oil that, in the days before electricity, lighted America's homes. A multi-million-dollar company, Standard Oil had achieved its position by a combination of shrewd business tactics and a ruthless approach to competition.

There were people who believed that the corruption that existed in trusts like the Standard Oil Company was proof that the whole concept of privately owned corporations was wrong. Ida disagreed with them. She felt it was not capitalism, but the unethical behavior of capitalists, that was at fault. She hoped that the *McClure's* series on trusts would prove it.

Ida had long been fascinated by the oil industry. When she was working for *The Chautauquan,* she had once tried to write a novel about it but had given it up as a bad job. The prospect of dealing with the subject now in a factual way seemed more suited to her talents. In fact, it sounded like a series she had been born to write. She had grown up surrounded by oil tanks and derricks. She had lived through her father's battles with the forerunner of Standard Oil, the South Improvement Company. Her brother, Will, worked for an independent oil company in Titusville and often talked about his own difficulties with the trust.

Ida was beginning to grow more and more fascinated by the idea. At this time Samuel McClure was in Europe, but she broached the subject of a series on the Standard Oil Company to the rest of the staff at their next editorial conference. They all shook their heads. It sounded dull. Could she make it interesting? Would anyone want to read it?

Ida, sure that the answers to both questions would

be yes, wrote an outline of the article and left it on John Phillips' desk. Phillips liked it, but he did not want to let Ida begin work on such a time-consuming project without first getting his partner's approval. The Chief, as McClure liked to be called, was still in Europe. "Go over," Phillips told Ida. "Show the outline to Sam and get his decision."

McClure and his wife, Hattie, were in Lausanne, Switzerland. Ida left to visit them in September 1901. It took her almost two weeks to get there. She planned on spending another week talking the project over with McClure, and if all went well, she would be back in New York, ready to go to work, in less than a month.

Ida, of course, had not reckoned on McClure's talent for disregarding other people's plans. He took one look at the outline and announced that he had to think it over. "Mrs. McClure and you and I will go to Greece for the winter," he told her. "We can discuss Standard Oil in Greece just as well as here."

Ida, scarcely settled into her room in Lausanne, soon found herself heading through northern Italy on the way to Greece. In Milan, however, McClure changed his mind once more. There was a resort nearby, called Salsomaggiore, that was noted for its remarkable mineral springs and mud baths. Nothing would do but that Ida and the McClures stop off for a sample of its curative waters. They had been at Salsomaggiore only a short time when McClure changed his mind still a third time. "There's no point in your staying here any longer," he told Ida abruptly. "Go back to New York and get started on that series."

Packing her trunk once more, Ida took the steamboat back to New York. She arrived in the middle of November and immediately began working on the book that would make her famous for all time— *The History of the Standard Oil Company.*

Chapter 10

Before she could actually begin writing her history of Standard Oil, Ida had to do a tremendous amount of research. The company had been in existence for more than thirty years. If she wanted to trace its development accurately, she would have to investigate its operations from the very beginning. She would need facts and figures about every aspect of the company's growth.

The most logical place to go for information about the Standard Oil Company was the company itself. Ida wrote to several of the executives in the New York offices on lower Broadway. They answered her politely but they would tell her very little.

Ida had expected as much. The Standard Oil Company had always been secretive about its methods of doing business. She knew, though, that many of the oil trust's activities were a matter of public record.

Ida Tarbell in 1904.
(BROWN BROTHERS)

Rouseville, Pennsylvania, in 1867 (MATHER COLLECTION,
DRAKE MUSEUM, TITUSVILLE, PENNSYLVANIA)

The Tarbell house, East Main Street, Titusville. In 1870 Frank Tarbell bought the Bonta House hotel at Pithole, had it torn down, and used the material to build this new home for the family.
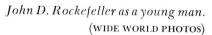
(MATHER COLLECTION, DRAKE MUSEUM,

TITUSVILLE, PENNSYLVANIA)

John D. Rockefeller as a young man.
(WIDE WORLD PHOTOS)

The staff of The Chautauquan *in 1888. Ida Tarbell is seated at the left.* (from TARBELL, *ALL IN THE DAY'S WORK*)

S.S.McClure

*Ida Tarbell at
her desk at*
McClure's Magazine.
(from TARBELL, *ALL IN
THE DAY'S WORK*)

Lincoln Steffens.
(BROWN BROTHERS)

Ray Stannard Baker.
(THE BETTMANN ARCHIVE)

*In 1883 a cartoonist portrayed railroad directors
"milking" their stockholders and the public.*
(THE BETTMANN ARCHIVE)

Standard Oil and other trusts as "the bosses of the Senate": a cartoon of 1893.   (THE BETTMANN ARCHIVE)

*John D. Rockefeller,
the Oil King.*
(THE BETTMANN ARCHIVE)

Henry H. Rogers.
(BROWN BROTHERS)

John D. Rockefeller.   (WIDE WORLD PHOTOS)

S.S.McClure at eighty-six, in the library of the Union League Club.

Ida Tarbell.

Almost from the day it was founded, Standard Oil had been under investigation by Congress and by the legislatures of the various states in which it operated. The testimony taken at these hearings alone provided a good insight into the company's tactics. The files of the newspapers and magazines that were published in the Oil Region would provide further details about Standard Oil's long-time war with the independent producers in the region. Still another source of information was the records of the various suits that individual oil refineries had brought against the monopoly in local courts.

Ida expected to find all the documents she needed without much difficulty. She thought it would simply be a matter of tracking down the necessary information and copying it into her notebooks. It turned out to be much more complicated.

Almost all the investigations of the Standard Oil Company had been published in pamphlet form, but the pamphlets had disappeared from the library shelves.

Ida consulted several librarians. They all shook their heads. "You'll never find them," they told her. "They've all been destroyed."

Most of the pamphlets had indeed been bought up by representatives of Standard Oil and subsequently burned. But whenever someone assured Ida that not a single copy of a certain document was available, she made it a firm policy to keep on looking. Invariably one would turn up in a private collection. More than once she found what she wanted by writing to her friend Adelaide Hasse. Miss Hasse, a member of the staff of the New York Public Library, was a genius at unearthing hard-to-find documents and buying them for the library's collection.

As the quest for information continued, Ida was appalled at the amount of time and money it was beginning to take. She was even more dismayed when she realized that she was never going to finish the job without an assistant to help her. Apologetically she approached Sam McClure and asked if she could hire one.

McClure, convinced that the series was going to cause a sensation, gave no thought to the extra expense. "Go ahead," he told her. "Hire anyone you want."

Ida knew exactly the kind of person she needed for the job. It would have to be a young man with a college education—bright, energetic, and above all, curious. Doing research, as she knew from her experience with Napoleon and Abraham Lincoln, was much like solving a puzzle. You had to get caught up in the excitement of finding the right pieces and fitting them into place.

Ida wanted someone who would work in Cleveland, the headquarters of the Standard Oil Company, so she wrote to three editors she knew in the Ohio city and asked them to recommend three young men. She then wrote to each of the candidates and asked them to find additional information about a not very important event. She would be in Cleveland in a few weeks, she told them, to see what they had turned up.

True to her word, Ida appeared soon afterward to check up on the results. Two of the young men turned in satisfactory pieces of research, but they showed no interest whatever in the subject and wanted only to collect their fee. Ida thanked them, paid them for their time, and sent them on their way.

The third young man came in bursting with excitement. He had not only found all the information she wanted, but had grown so absorbed in the subject that he could hardly wait to find out more. Ida hired him on the spot. The researcher's name was John Siddall, and, by coincidence, he worked for *The Chautauquan,* which had moved its office from Meadville to Cleveland a few years before. Siddall turned out to be such a good choice for the job that when his research on the Standard Oil series was finished, S. S. McClure invited him to come to New York and become an editor on *McClure's.*

As Ida sifted through the mountain of evidence that she and John Siddall were amassing against Standard Oil, Ida saw that John D. Rockefeller's rise to power had started with a system of preferential rates called rebates. This was the same practice that had triggered the furor Ida remembered from her girlhood.

The South Improvement Company, which had caused the trouble in the Oil Region then, was made up of five refining companies; the largest was

Standard Oil. Under the leadership of John D. Rockefeller, the organization made secret agreements with three railroads—the Pennsylvania, the Erie, and the New York Central. According to the terms of their contract, the refiners who belonged to the South Improvement Company would be charged only forty cents a barrel for shipping crude oil. Twenty-six other oil refiners in Cleveland, competitors of Rockefeller's, were not included in the deal. The railroads agreed to charge these outsiders eighty cents a barrel for their oil shipments.

The spectacular difference in shipping costs made it virtually impossible for the independent refiners to compete with the larger oil company. Twenty-one of the twenty-six eventually sold out to Rockefeller.

During the last half of the nineteenth century it was not unusual for the railroads to enter into rebate agreements with businessmen. They overcharged the public anyway, so they weren't really losing money. Moreover, lower shipping rates enabled large companies to undersell their competitors—thus increasing their own business and the business of the railroads as well.

John D. Rockefeller added a new and even more vicious twist to the rebate system. It was called the drawback. With drawbacks, companies not only received preferential rates; they were also allowed to collect the overcharges that were paid to the railroads by their rivals. It was an easy matter for Rockefeller to arrange the drawbacks. Standard Oil controlled the railroads. Rockefeller owned most of their stock, and his executives sat on the board of directors of every major line in the country.

In addition to rebates and drawbacks, Standard Oil had other equally ugly ways of doing business. John Sidall found a woman in Cleveland named Mrs. Backus who had been married to a refinery owner. When her husband died unexpectedly, the widow went to John D. Rockefeller and offered to sell him the business so she would have enough money to support herself and her three children. Rockefeller assured her, with tears in his eyes, that he would do everything in his power to help her. Then he turned around and paid her only $79,000 for the refinery—$120,000 less than it had originally cost.

Ida and her assistant talked to another Clevelander, a lubricating-oil manufacturer who bought his raw petroleum from Standard Oil. The man had a contract that allowed him to purchase eighty-five barrels of oil a day, but one day he was abruptly informed that he was allowed only twelve barrels. At the same time, both the price of the oil and the cost of shipping it were doubled. The man was soon forced out of business and ended up selling his plant for a mere $15,000. He had paid $41,000 for it.

These tactics were mild compared to some of the other things John D. Rockefeller's agents stooped to. In Buffalo, New York, the owners of the Vacuum Oil Company, which had been bought up by Standard Oil, were determined to ruin a rival concern called the Buffalo Lubricating Works. Representatives of Vacuum Oil bribed the Buffalo's chief mechanic to make the fire in one of its tanks so hot that the safety valve blew off and 175 barrels of oil were ruined.

When the Buffalo Lubricating Works still refused to shut down, the Vacuum men offered the chief mechanic $4,000 to give up his job and move to California. The mechanic accepted the offer, and since no one else in the company knew enough about machinery to continue its operations, business at the Buffalo Lubricating Works quickly ground to a halt.

The mechanic later admitted the plot, and three officials of Standard Oil were brought to trial on charges of conspiring to put the Buffalo Works out of business. All three were acquitted, and the owners of the Vacuum Oil Company got off with only a modest fine.

Ida knew, and hoped to prove in her book, that Standard Oil was not above bribing witnesses, jurors, and even judges to secure a verdict in its favor. It was perfectly consistent with John D. Rockefeller's willingness to sacrifice anything and anyone in his pursuit of profits and power.

Chapter 11

Ida was about halfway along in her research when Samuel McClure broke the news to his readers that the magazine would soon publish *The History of the Standard Oil Company*. The announcement gave a further boost to her efforts.

Mark Twain, who was a friend of McClure's, buttonholed the publisher one day and demanded to know what kind of history it was going to be. McClure shrugged. "You'll have to ask Miss Tarbell," he murmured.

The reason for Twain's interest soon became apparent. Another of his good friends was Henry Rogers, one of John D. Rockefeller's vice-presidents at Standard Oil.

The writer and the businessman had known each other for some time, and when Twain found himself practically penniless after the panic of 1893, he appealed to Rogers for help. Rogers immediately took charge of his investments, rescued him from bankruptcy, and remained his close friend and financial adviser until he died. Now Rogers had obviously asked the author to serve as his go-between with S. S. McClure. "Would Miss Tarbell be willing to talk to Mr. Rogers?" Mark Twain wanted to know.

"I'm sure she'd be delighted," McClure replied.

Ida was more than delighted. It was an opportunity she had not dared to hope for. With Mark Twain's help an interview was arranged at Mr. Rogers' imposing New York town house.

Ida's teeth were chattering as she walked up Fifth Avenue and across Fifty-seventh Street to the address Twain had given her. The chattering might have been caused by the blustery January weather, but Ida was more inclined to blame it on her nerves. She had never met a capain of industry before.

Would he be ferocious and overbearing? Cold and mean? Or just unpleasant? For an instant Ida hesitated. Then she took a deep breath and resolutely reached for the big brass knocker on the door. She had already become acquainted with the Standard Oil Company on paper. Now it was time to meet it face to face.

Ida's nervousness vanished the instant Henry Rogers shook her hand. He was about sixty years old, a tall handsome man with a warm smile and alert dark eyes. His thick grey hair, bushy eyebrows, and drooping mustache reminded her of Mark Twain. He appeared to have Twain's gift for laughter as well. Ida knew that Mark Twain despised everything Standard Oil stood for, but she was beginning to see why he numbered one of its vice-presidents among his friends.

Henry Rogers showed his guest into his dark wood-paneled library and invited her to sit down. The first thing he wanted to know was when and where she had developed such an interest in oil.

"On the flats and hills of Rouseville," Ida replied.

Henry Rogers' dark eyes lit up with a flash of recognition. "Of course," he exclaimed, "Tarbell's Tank Shops! I knew your father. I could put my finger on the spot where those tanks stood."

Rogers was originally from New England, he explained to Ida, but the news of Colonel Edwin Drake's oil wells had prompted him to come to Pennsylvania as a young man. He had gone into the refining business in Rouseville, married, and put the first $1,000 he managed to save into a home on the hillside above the flatlands, not far from the Tarbells'. "It was a little white house," Rogers recalled, "with a high peaked roof."

Ida remembered it quite clearly. It was one of the few good-looking homes in Rouseville. "As a child I thought it was the prettiest house in the world," she told her beaming host.

The two former neighbors began reminiscing about the hillside where they had both lived. Ida's house had been separated from the Rogerses' by a ravine with a narrow path on either side. Ida had often played along the path on her side of the ravine, catching butterflies and moths or hunting for ferns and wild flowers.

Henry Rogers, almost twenty years her senior, had different memories of his own path. He had been a young husband then. "Up that path," he said, "I used to carry our washing every Monday morning and go for it every Saturday night. Probably I've seen you hunting flowers on your side of the ravine. How beautiful it was! I was never happier!"

Ida was stunned to find herself having a pleasant chat about the Pennsylvania countryside with one of the nation's most notorious robber barons. Rogers had a reputation for being cold as steel in business, but socially he was one of the most charming men Ida had ever met. Even when the conversation finally got around to the real reason for her visit—the history of the Standard Oil Company—Henry Rogers was no less affable. He was curious, however, to know where she was planning to get the information for the story.

"From newspapers and public records," Ida told him. "I'm beginning with the investigations of the South Improvement Company."

Henry Rogers had not been a member of Standard Oil at the time of the South Improvement Company's conspiracy. He had, in fact, been one of the most outspoken foes of the arrangement. "It was an outrageous business," he told Ida. "Rockefeller made a big mistake there."

Ida knew that John D. Rockefeller had made other equally outrageous "mistakes" since then, many of them with the assistance of Henry Rogers.

But she decided to say nothing about them for the present.

If there was any information she wanted about the Standard Oil Company, Henry Rogers told his guest, he would be happy to give it to her. Ida was taken aback by his offer. "So far no one in the company has been willing to talk to me," she said.

Rogers smiled pleasantly. "We've changed our policy," he said. "We're giving out information now."

The change in policy, Ida suspected, had been established that very moment. Again she said nothing. Henry Rogers' cooperation was too valuable to risk losing.

Ida Tarbell spent nearly two hours with Henry Rogers that January afternoon. They talked about the history of the oil business. They discussed rebates and pipelines and even went over a list of some of the companies that had been gobbled up by Standard Oil.

Rogers apologized for nothing. He was more interested in convincing Ida of the size and scope of John D. Rockefeller's achievements. He pointed out how well organized the Standard Oil Company was, how cleverly Mr. Rockefeller had planned his moves, and how methodically he had executed them.

The more they talked, the more at home Ida felt with him. Although she was sure he had done many things that she considered immoral, she could not help admiring his frankness and good humor. In later years she called Henry Rogers "as fine a pirate as ever flew his flag in Wall Street."

Before they said good-bye, the two ex-Pennsylvanians made an agreement that before Ida wrote about any of the legal cases the Standard Oil Company had been involved in, she would first talk to Rogers. He would provide her with further documents and arguments to explain Standard Oil's side of the question.

"Would you be willing to come to my office? It might be a little more convenient," he said.

"Certainly," Ida replied.

"Would you talk with Mr. Rockefeller?" he inquired.

"Of course," Ida said.

Rogers seemed surprised to find her so agreeable. "Well," he muttered uncertainly, "I'll try to arrange it."

Ida felt obliged to make it clear to Henry Rogers that she was perfectly willing to listen to his side of Standard Oil's story, but in the end, she would have to form her own opinions about the company. "It's my history," she told him, "so my judgment must prevail."

Henry Rogers nodded. "I suppose," he said cheerfully as he showed her to the door, "we'll just have to stand it."

Chapter 12

When Ida Tarbell had first talked over her history of the Standard Oil Company with S. S. McClure in Salsomaggiore, Italy, they agreed that it would run for three installments. By the time McClure got back from Europe, he had decided that six installments would be better.

The first one appeared in November 1902. The staff members who had at first greeted the idea so unenthusiastically were chagrined when they saw the finished piece. *The History of the Standard Oil Company* was as exciting as a suspense story. Time and again, readers wrote in to say that they were anxiously awaiting the next installment.

Samuel McClure had worked out a foolproof method for pleasing the public. Whenever he launched a new series, he watched carefully to see if people were interested. If the magazine's circulation fell, the series was dropped after one or two installments. If the circulation rose, the series was stretched out for as many installments as the material permitted.

Although his writers were often disappointed when a series failed to catch on with the public, they never held it against S. S. McClure. He paid them generously for their work and allowed them as much time as they wanted to complete their assignments.

Ida wrote her Standard Oil history so that each chapter was a separate article and the whole series could be discontinued at any point if the readers' interest started to wane. She needn't have bothered. The enthusiasm for the story was so great that the series continued for almost two years and became one of the longest pieces of writing ever published in a national magazine.

Ida had not forgotten her agreement with Henry Rogers. For months, she made regular visits to his office at 26 Broadway. The visits were an adventure in themselves. Ida was amused at the way she was always escorted in and out of Rogers' office through a secret corridor, and she was fascinated by his efficient, stony-faced private secretary. She knew almost as much about the business as Henry Rogers did and was rumored to be earning the staggering sum of $10,000 a year.

Henry Rogers remained as frank and good-humored as he had been at their first meeting. He was not offended in the slightest when Ida insisted on discussing some of the occasions when he and his associates had flouted the law. Once she presented him with some testimony he had given in court that was an outright lie. "They had no business prying into my private affairs," he snapped. When she asked him about rebates, he was equally unrepentant. "Somebody else would have taken them if we hadn't," he said with a shrug.

Their talks were usually friendly and informal, but occasionally one of them would become angry. When this happened, the other was quick to change the subject. One day Ida was discussing a man who worked for Standard Oil. She had accumulated evidence that proved him guilty of a number of cunning and deceitful maneuvers. Henry Rogers defended the man and Ida became infuriated. "He's a liar and a hypocrite and you know it!" she cried.

Henry Rogers walked over to the window and made a great pretense of studying the sky over lower Broadway. "I think it's going to rain," he finally announced with a grin.

Henry Rogers had a reputation for being a daring investor. He had put huge sums of money into some very dubious stocks, but most of his investments had paid off handsomely. One day Ida told him about the time there had been a sudden rise in the market and everyone in town had rushed to buy stocks. Ida was attending Titusville High School then. Caught up in the fever, she had asked her father to give her $100 so that she, too, could try her luck in the market.

Frank Tarbell had refused. He was convinced that speculating in the stock market was just as much gambling as shooting dice or playing poker. To him it was morally wrong.

Henry Rogers chuckled. A born gambler, he loved the excitement of playing for high stakes. "I find a poker game when the stock market's closed," he confessed.

Henry Rogers and Ida Tarbell had disagreements about several of the legal cases Standard Oil had been involved in. Usually they managed to settle them amicably, but one day Ida came to the office with some information that left Henry Rogers white with rage.

In studying the testimony against the Standard Oil Company in various court records, Ida was constantly coming across charges by independent oil producers that their shipments had been sabotaged. Time and again they maintained that their cars were being sidetracked; oil, lost or destroyed, never arrived at its destination. The producers insisted that the monopoly was paying off the railroad freight clerks to report on how much oil was being shipped by their rivals and where it was going.

At first Ida was dubious about the charges. As she knew from her own experience, a certain amount of spying on competitors was inevitable in business. The editors at *McClure's* were always on the alert to see what *Harper's* or *The Atlantic* were up to. She knew too that the independent producers despised Standard Oil so thoroughly that they believed them capable of almost any kind of wrongdoing.

Then, quite accidentally, Ida discovered that the charges against the company were true. Her information came through a teen-aged boy who worked in the office of one of Standard Oil's refineries. Each month he was assigned the job of burning a large stack of office records. The boy accepted the task as part of his duties until, one night, he happened to see a familiar name on one of the papers he was stuffing into the fire. It was the name of an independent oil refiner who taught Sunday school in the church the boy attended.

The young man began taking a closer look at the papers he had been told to destroy. His friend's name appeared again and again, and after some weeks he put together enough of the records to realize what they were. The Standard Oil Company had a complete file on every shipment of oil that left the man's refinery. The information came from the railroad office and was passed on to railroad agents along the routes with orders to see that the shipments went astray.

The young man was horrified at what he had discovered. He stopped burning the papers on which the oilman's name appeared and instead put them aside and took them to him. The man, who had been following Ida's articles in *McClure's,* brought the evidence to her at once. There was no question that the documents were authentic. They fitted in perfectly with all the testimony Ida had read against the Standard Oil Company.

On her next visit to 26 Broadway, Ida told Henry Rogers what she had found out and asked him for an explanation. Rogers shook his head.

"We do everything we legally and fairly can to find out what our competitors are up to," he said, "just as you do in *McClure's Magazine*. But this accusation is ridiculous. It's just a lot of nonsense."

When Rogers refused to discuss the matter any further, Ida went ahead and, using fictitious names, printed the information she had received. She had an appointment with Henry Rogers some weeks later. When she arrived in his office, a copy of *McClure's* lay open on the table.

"Where did you get that stuff?" Rogers roared, pointing to the article about the sabotage.

"I can't tell you," Ida replied stiffly.

Up until then, Henry Rogers had been happy to help Ida. He did not approve of what she was writing but he knew that she had gotten much of her material from public records. Part of the book would include old evidence from lawsuits and investigations that Standard Oil had already managed to wiggle out of.

Rogers hoped that his cooperation would persuade Ida not to be too hard on Standard Oil in the rest of the book, but he also had enough confidence in the company's efficiency to believe that she would never get her hands on any information that could be used against them in some future trial.

Ida's story about the sabotaged oil shipments took

Henry Rogers by complete surprise. Moreover, her refusal to reveal its source meant that he had no way of retaliating against the employees who had been careless enough to let such important documents go astray. Ida could easily understand his rage at this unexpected turn of events. She was not the least bit surprised when the visit proved to be the last she ever made to the offices of the Standard Oil Company.

Henry Rogers had been very helpful in arranging interviews with some of the most important men in the company, but every time Ida reminded him of his promise to introduce her to John D. Rockefeller, he balked. Rockefeller was busy, or out of town, or not feeling well. Finally, Rogers came right out and told her what she had suspected all along. John D. Rockefeller refused to see her.

As her work on the history continued, Ida grew more and more curious about the founder of the industrial empire she was writing about. She remembered something Ralph Waldo Emerson had said: "An institution is the lengthened shadow of one man." Ida had studied the institution; now she wanted to study the man.

She already knew the basic facts of his life. Rockefeller had grown up on a farm in upstate New York. His family moved to Ohio, and in 1855, at the age of sixteen, the future millionaire went to work as a bookkeeper. Thrifty and industrious, he soon decided to go into business for himself. By 1865 he had become a partner in a Cleveland oil refinery. Ten years later he was the dominant figure in the industry.

Having given up all hope of meeting John D. Rockefeller, Ida thought she at least ought to see what he looked like. Her resourceful assistant, John Siddall, came to her aid. He discovered that John D. Rockefeller was scheduled to give a talk to the Sunday School classes at the church he attended in Cleveland. Siddall decided to take Ida to the talk and to the church service after it. "I'll see that we have good seats," he promised. "You'll have a chance to watch him in action."

Ida and John Siddall spent two hours at Rockefeller's church that October Sunday in 1903. Rockefeller sat at the front of the Sunday School room, where they could study him at their leisure. Ida was struck by his enormous head, long sharp nose, and thin tight mouth. His eyes fascinated her even more. Small and colorless, they darted nervously around the room taking in every detail.

At first sight, Ida thought John D. Rockefeller looked old and feeble, but when he rose to speak, she was impressed by the tremendous sense of power he exuded. His voice was strong and he was obviously sincere about what he was saying. Ida could not help being amused, however, that the topic he selected for his Sunday School speech had the ring of big business in it. He talked about dividends—the dividends of righteousness.

After the talk, Ida and John Siddall slipped out of

the classroom and found a place in the church's choir loft where they could watch the oil magnate in the congregation below.

"Well, what did you think of him?" John Siddall demanded when the service was over.

Ida shook her head. "In spite of all his power and wealth, he seemed nervous and afraid," she said. "I found myself feeling sorry for him."

When Ida had first started working on *The History of the Standard Oil Company,* almost everyone she met warned her that it was a dangerous undertaking. The company detested public scrutiny, and they were quick to take revenge on anyone who tried to pry into their operations. Even Frank Tarbell was leery of seeing his daughter get involved in the project. "Don't do it, Ida," he told her. "They'll ruin the magazine."

Ida, of course, went ahead anyway. Neither she nor *McClure's* was ruined. The only penalties she suffered were some snide references to herself as Ida Tarbarrel and her own mixed feelings of disgust and despair when the book was finished. She had seen too many tragic injustices and talked to too many people whose lives had been ruined by clashes with Standard Oil.

One experience that affected her deeply was a visit she had with John D. Rockefeller's brother Frank. Ida knew that the two men had had a quarrel a few years earlier, but she had never bothered to investigate it. It was a family affair; she was writing a business history. Then one day she received a message that Frank Rockefeller wanted to arrange a secret meeting with her.

John Siddall took care of the details as efficiently as he had managed their visit to the Cleveland church. Ida, smuggled into Rockefeller's office under an assumed name, found the man in a terrible state of agitation. Angrily denouncing his brother for cheating him out of stock in the Standard Oil Company, he insisted that Ida hear all the details.

It seemed that Frank Rockefeller had organized a shipping business some years before. He had borrowed money from his brother John to finance it, offering the stock he owned in Standard Oil as collateral. When the panic of 1893 erupted, Frank Rockefeller had been unable to meet the payments on the loan. John had foreclosed and kept the stock, which had increased in value and would have made his brother a wealthy man.

John D. Rockefeller had been within his legal rights in the transaction, and Ida was sure that his conscience was clear. From her brief visit with Frank Rockefeller, she could see that he liked to spend his earnings to enjoy life. John D. Rockefeller considered that type of man frivolous and not to be trusted with large sums of money.

Ida was shaken by the depths of Frank Rockefeller's bitterness against his brother. He refused to let any of his children be buried in the Rockefeller cemetery plot. "They shall not lie in the same enclosure with John D. Rockefeller," he cried, furiously pounding his fist on the desk.

The experience made Ida happy to be finished with *The History of the Standard Oil Company.* "Now I can escape back to the library and write about people who are dead and gone," she told John Phillips. "Maybe they've done things I don't approve of, but it won't bother me as much to read about them."

Chapter 13

The last chapter of *The History of the Standard Oil Company* appeared in *McClure's* in October 1904. A few weeks later the complete series was published as a book. Later historians of the oil monopoly have praised Ida Tarbell for her accuracy and thoroughness, but a few scholars have protested that the book's portrayal of John D. Rockefeller was unfair.

Ida had depicted him as such a money-hungry ogre that another writer, Henry Demarest Lloyd, told her, "When you get through with Johnnie, I don't think there will be much left of him except something resembling one of his own grease spots."

Lloyd was right. Rockefeller's image was permanently damaged in the public mind. But Ida had no regrets about her characterization of Standard Oil's founder. Her conclusions were based on solid evidence, and she saw no reason to apologize for them.

Soon after Ida's book was published, John D. Rockefeller made a number of substantial contributions to charity. Many people suggested that his gifts were prompted by a desire to improve his tarnished reputation. They congratulated Ida for "opening the Rockefeller purse." Ida refused to take any credit. "John D. Rockefeller has always been a generous man," she insisted.

Even during his days as a struggling young bookkeeper the millionaire-to-be had regularly set aside 10 percent of his salary for charity. He had continued this tithing, as the practice is called, as his income increased. He founded the University of Chicago in 1889 and the Rockefeller Institute for Medical Research in 1901. By 1904 he had given away some $35 million. If his gifts were greater after that, Ida always pointed out, it was because his wealth was greater as well.

The fact remained, however, that after *The History of the Standard Oil Company* appeared, John D. Rockefeller went to great lengths to improve his reputation. He hired the country's first publicity man, Ivy Lee, and instead of concealing his philanthropies as he often had done in the past, he allowed his name to be used as frequently as possible. Thanks to Ivy Lee's efforts the Rockefeller image was considerably—but never completely—improved.

The History of the Standard Oil Company made a tremendous impact on the nation. It was praised in sermons and newspaper editorials, and more than one politician used it to support his stand against big business. From Standard Oil itself there was only a loud silence. One of Rockefeller's assistants suggested writing a reply to Ida Tarbell's charges, but the oilman refused. He didn't even like to hear her name mentioned in his presence. "Not a word," he decreed, "not a word about that misguided woman."

A few company stalwarts decided to retaliate by reprinting 5 million copies of a book that tried to refute Ida's evidence. They distributed them to teachers, journalists, ministers, and public officials all over the country. Several of the editors at *McClure's* managed to get hold of some copies, which they jokingly presented to Ida each year on her birthday or for Christmas.

The reprint was one of the few adverse criticisms of the book. Elsewhere it was proclaimed a journalistic triumph and its author applauded as one of the most courageous women in America. She was called a modern Joan of Arc and hailed as the "Terror of the Trusts."

The effects of Ida's disclosures began to be felt almost at once. In Missouri a suit was filed against Standard Oil charging the company with trying to fix prices and destroy competition. Soon after that, President Theodore Roosevelt's newly created Department of Commerce and Labor went into action. One of its divisions, the Bureau of Corporations, accused Standard Oil of taking secret rebates from the railroads. The United States Attorney General subsequently began prosecuting the company under the

Sherman Anti-Trust Act, which held that any monopoly in restraint of trade was illegal.

The first tangible result of the book came in 1906, when Congress passed the Hepburn Act. The law made the penalties for rebates so severe that the practice at last died out. In 1909 a federal circuit court held that the Standard Oil Company was in violation of the Sherman Anti-Trust Act. Two years later the decision was affirmed by the United States Supreme Court, and the mammoth monopoly was dissolved into thirty-eight separate and smaller corporations.

The Supreme Court ruling condemned Standard Oil for "unreasonable" restraint of trade but it also acknowledged a fact that Ida, too, had regretfully come to accept. The era of the giant corporation was here to stay. The Court's decision implied that trusts could be tolerated as long as they did not engage in ruthless extermination of their rivals. It urged large companies to work together with small ones in their mutual interests.

The January 1903 issue of *McClure's* had marked an important milestone in the history of journalism. The issue contained three major articles—an exposé of corruption in Minneapolis by Lincoln Steffens, an investigation of labor unions by Ray Stannard Baker, and a chapter from Ida Tarbell's *History of the Standard Oil Company*.

The magazine's reception had been nothing short of sensational. *McClure's* circulation had soared. Before long, articles attacking America's political, economic, and social ills began to appear in every other magazine in the country.

Samuel Hopkins Adams exposed food adulteration and the frauds in patent-medicine advertising in *Collier's*. David Graham Phillips attacked the shady deals between senators and businessmen in *Cosmopolitan*. Upton Sinclair wrote a novel, *The Jungle,* that decried the wretched conditions in Chicago's meat-packing plants.

Eventually other, less responsible journalists began capitalizing on the new trend. Their attacks were not as carefully researched and documented as those of the original reformers. Many, filled with half-truths, were published solely in the interests of sensationalism.

In response to the public clamor they aroused, President Theodore Roosevelt had taken up several of the early magazine crusades and persuaded Congress to enact some badly needed reforms; but as the journalists' preoccupation with business and political evils continued he grew more and more unhappy. The press, he felt, was undermining the nation's morale.

At a speech before the Gridiron Club in March 1906, Roosevelt condemned the magazine writers for looking only at the bad side of things. He compared them to a character in John Bunyan's famous book *Pilgrim's Progress*: "the Man with the Muckrake, the man who could look no way but downward with the muckrake in his hand; who was offered a

celestial crown for his muckrake but who would neither look up nor regard the crown he was offered
but continued to rake to himself the filth of the
floor."

The speech was supposed to be off the record, but
the rumor soon started that Roosevelt had attacked
some of the country's leading writers. The president
tried to explain his position in a letter to Ray Stannard Baker. "I want to let in light and air but I do
not want to let in sewer gas," he wrote. "If a room is
fetid and the windows are bolted, I am perfectly
willing to knock out the windows but I would not
knock a hole in the drain pipe."

A few weeks later Roosevelt spoke at the dedica-
tion of the cornerstone of the House of Representatives Office Building. The president once again condemned reckless and irresponsible exposés, but this
time he also praised the writers who were attacking
legitimate social ills.

Which writers were muckrakers and which were
not, the president did not say, so the word was soon
applied to any writer who was working on behalf of
reform. The insult was transformed into a term of
approval, and Ida, who had at first resented being
called a muckraker, came to accept the title as a
badge of distinction.

Chapter 14

In the winter of 1904, while Ida was still rejoicing over the successful completion of *The History of the Standard Oil Company*, she received some sad news from Titusville. Frank Tarbell was ill, and the doctor could hold out no hope for his recovery.

For the next few months Ida spent many long weekends commuting back and forth to Pennsylvania. Frank Tarbell had been a friend as well as a father, and it was heartbreaking to see him struggling against his long, painful illness. When he finally died in the spring of 1905, Ida could only feel grateful that he would suffer no more.

Ida did not feel the full impact of her father's death until after he had been laid to rest in Woodlawn Cemetery. By then there was no time to give way to her grief. Oil had been discovered in Kansas, and S. S. McClure expected his leading authority on the subject to cover the story for *McClure's*.

Wildcatters had been drilling for oil in that part

of the country for years. When they finally found it, Kansas and its neighbor, Oklahoma, went crazy. Ida, who could remember some of the excitement of the oil boom in Pennsylvania, was fascinated by the new discovery. Oil was all anyone could talk about. Oil wells and stocks in oil companies were selling like mad. They were all going to make their owners millionaires.

To show how ridiculous the oil fever had become, a group of young Kansans got together and as a practical joke sent out letters offering shares in a nonexistent oil field. They were immediately swamped with replies from people beggging for an opportunity to invest. Checks and money orders poured in at such a rate that the young men were thrown into a panic. Fearful that they would be sent to jail as swindlers, they finally had to throw themselves on the mercy of some older men, who helped them out of the predicament by putting the money into a legitimate oil field.

Ida's ten days in southeastern Kansas and Oklahoma were a new experience for her. Driving across the prairie one afternoon in a buckboard, she was startled to see an ominous dark cloud rolling toward her from the distance. It looked like smoke, but the man who was driving the buckboard knew better. "It's a dust storm," he told his perplexed passenger. "Put your head down and close your eyes."

The man loosened the horses' reins, and the animals, obviously used to such emergencies, braced themselves against each other and put their heads down almost to the ground. Ida and her companion did the same. Seconds later, the huge dark cloud engulfed them. The dust was so thick that Ida could hardly get her breath.

Fortunately, the cloud passed in seconds. When Ida stood up to look after it, she found that she was covered with fine black dust. It was all over her clothes, her face, and her hair. Worst of all, the storm had contaminated the local water supply, and it was ten days before she had enough clean water in which to take a bath.

Ida had come to the new oil lands as an ordinary reporter, but she soon found she was being treated as a celebrity. When she arrived in Tulsa, Oklahoma, the editor of the local newspaper invited her over to his office to interview her for a front-page story. "I think I should warn you," he told her when they were finished talking, "you're in for a surprise."

A large brass band organized by a group of happy-go-lucky oil workers had arrived in Tulsa that morning. "They want something to celebrate," the editor told her, "and when they heard that you were in town, they decided to come up and welcome you. They want a speech."

Ida was horrified. She couldn't possibly make a speech on two minutes' notice. "You've got to get me out of this," she pleaded.

The newspaperman laughed. "There's no way to escape," he said as the blare of trumpets sounded in the street outside. "Here they are."

Thinking quickly, Ida reached into her purse and

pulled out some dollar bills. "Quick," she ordered the editor, "go buy me two boxes of the best cigars you can find."

When Ida came out on the sidewalk to greet her serenaders, she discovered half the population of Tulsa was there ahead of her. They were as amused by her consternation as they were by the concert. To Ida's relief the editor returned with the cigars before the music was over. When the last note sounded and the musicians called for a speech, she stepped into the street and handed each of them a cigar. As she had hoped, they much preferred a smoke to a speech. Thanking her with a rousing blast from their horns, they went marching off down the street.

Ida's job at *McClure's* was the most satisfying one she had ever held. She was deeply disturbed when, after investing a dozen years of her life in the magazine, it became obvious that she could no longer go on working for S. S. McClure.

McClure had driven himself so hard to achieve success as a publisher that he had become a sick man. He was troubled by insomnia, indigestion, and an assortment of similar ailments that kept him in and out of the hospital or traveling back and forth to Europe.

The magazine, under John Phillips' experienced eye, continued to provide him with a substantial income, but McClure missed the excitement of work. A restless, energetic man, he was not happy unless he was thinking up new ideas and creating new enterprises. Sometimes he would return from one of his rest cures in Europe with some first-rate ideas. More often his brainstorms made his staff wonder if he was really the genius they had once thought him.

In 1906 McClure returned to the office with the most grandiose plan he had yet devised. He was going to organize a company that would publish a new magazine, *McClure's Universal Journal*. The magazine would be part of a vast business enterprise that would also include a book-publishing firm, a bank, and a life insurance company. All of these would be promoted in the magazine.

The editors at *McClure's* were appalled at their chief's idea. It was not only shaky as a financial venture, but it would make *McClure's Universal Journal* nothing more than a publicity organ for its own corporate empire. The opportunities for corruption and mismanagement would be endless.

McClure's new company was against everything his original magazine had ever stood for. It was madness. Ida told him point-blank that she would have nothing to do with it. John Phillips went to his old friend and tried to persuade him to give up the scheme. McClure would not hear of it, and Phillips reluctantly announced that their partnership was dissolved.

Ida Tarbell could not imagine the magazine without John Phillips. She, too, resigned, and was soon joined by Ray Stannard Baker, Lincoln Steffens, John Siddall, and the managing editor, Albert Boyden.

The six staff members had known each other for

years. They had argued over articles and laughed over lunch. They were friends as well as co-workers.

Ida and John Phillips remembered when *McClure's* had occupied only a small suite of offices at 743 Broadway. The others had joined them after the magazine moved to more spacious quarters on Lexington Avenue, and they had all followed it in still another move to a larger and more prestigious building on East Twenty-third Street on the south side of elegant Madison Square. Together they had watched *McClure's* develop and prosper, and they knew that they could rightfully claim much of the responsibility for its success.

On their last day the sixsome glumly cleaned out their desks and left the Twenty-third Street offices together. Reluctant to say good-bye to each other, they wandered over to Madison Square Park and sat down on a bench. It was the end of an era for all of them.

Now what's going to become of us? Ida wondered.

Chapter 15

Within a few weeks, Ida and her associates from *McClure's* were offered the ownership of another publication, *Frank Leslie's Illustrated Monthly,* which had recently changed its name to *The American Magazine.* They formed a corporation, bought it, and six months later, in October 1906, published their first issue.

Ida was now close to her fiftieth birthday. Except for a few streaks of grey in her dark brown hair she showed little sign of growing old. Her figure was trim, her step lively, and her reporter's eye as keen as it had ever been. Besides taking on the job of contributing editor on *The American Magazine,* she had also become involved in a new interest—a home of her own.

In the years since her graduation from Allegheny College, Ida had had many temporary homes. First there was Poland, Ohio; then Meadville, Pennsylvania; then Paris, Washington, and finally New

York. But no matter where she lived or worked, Ida's heart remained in the Oil Region. Home was still the old house in Titusville with its fragrant garden and tower-room hideaway.

Ida loved to go back and visit with her family, but unfortunately the five-hundred-mile trip was too exhausting to make more than three or four times a year. Still a small-town girl at heart, Ida felt the need to get away from New York more often.

One day, some friends who had a home in Connecticut happened to mention an old farmhouse that was for sale near Danbury. When they took Ida to see it, she was strongly tempted to buy it. Before making up her mind, however, she decided to invite another of *The American's* editors, Albert Boyden, up to see it. She had great respect for Bert's opinions and she was anxious to hear what he would have to say.

Bert Boyden took one look at the sturdy oak trees around the house and the crooked stream that meandered gaily across one corner of the property. "Buy it," he ordered at once. And buy it, Ida did.

Her new home was an abandoned forty-acre farm on Rock House Road in the tiny village of Bethel. Less than a hundred miles from the city, it was the perfect spot for a weekend retreat. The house was a bit ramshackle, and the land hadn't been tended for years, but Ida didn't care. It was just a place to relax in.

On closer inspection, however, the new owner realized that her vacation home was going to absorb far more of her attention and money than she had anticipated. The roof leaked and had to be reshingled. When spring came she discovered that if she was going to sit outdoors and enjoy her country surroundings, the underbrush would have to be cleared and the grass mowed. Before long, Ida was not only refurbishing the old house, she was rejuvenating the farm as well. The fields were plowed and the orchards pruned; a cow and some horses appeared in the pasture; a pig and half a dozen chickens moved into the barn. A hired man was entrusted with the job of actually running the farm, but Ida took a lively interest in everything that went on there. Once she even put off buying a new evening dress and spent the money for a load of fertilizer instead.

Besides Noble and Ella Hoggson, the friends who had introduced her to Bethel, Ida found many congenial neighbors in Connecticut. The writer and editor Jeanette Gilder, whose brother edited *The Century Magazine,* lived nearby, and soon after Ida moved in, Mark Twain built a house not far away. Ida's mother, her sister Sarah, and Will and his wife, Ella, came to stay with her at least once a year. Her friends from *The American* were more frequent visitors.

Ida had expected to find peace and quiet in the country, but instead her social life in Connecticut was even livelier than it was in New York. It took all the self-discipline she could muster to continue working in spite of it.

Ida was sure that her friendship with Henry Rog-

136

ers had ended the day she confronted him with evidence of his company's plots to destroy their competitors' oil shipments. His name was often in the newspapers, however, and she followed his activities with great interest. At one point, Rogers was involved in an attempt to create a monopoly in the copper industry. The move set off a vicious business war much like the ones Standard Oil had fought with some of its early rivals.

Rogers was also guilty of some unethical speculations in the stock market, which were exposed in a series of articles by Thomas Lawson in *Everybody's Magazine*. The series had thrown Rogers into such a frenzy of rage that he threatened to drive the magazine out of business.

Before he could do anything, Henry Rogers suffered a stroke that left him an invalid for most of the summer of 1907. When he recovered there were other problems to contend with. The panic of 1907 was causing some tremendous upheavals in the stock market.

One afternoon in November, while the panic was still wreaking its havoc on the nation's banks and businesses, Ida was standing on a Fifth Avenue corner waiting to cross the street. Suddenly she saw someone waving to her from a passing automobile. She peered in and spied Henry Rogers smiling at her from the back seat.

Ida mentioned her brief glimpse of her old friend to John Phillips as soon as she got back to the office. "Why don't you try and see him?" Phillips said promptly. "If he'll talk about some of the things that are going on in the business world, you'll have a great story."

Would Henry Rogers see her? Ida thought it would be futile to even try. But then she remembered the wave and the smile. Perhaps she and Henry Rogers were still friends after all. That afternoon Ida sat down and wrote Rogers a note. His reply came back promptly. Would Ida stop in to see him at his house on Fifty-seventh Street?

Ida found her former neighbor from Rouseville as good-humored and straightforward as ever. He even joked about his recent financial losses. "You see," he said, as he turned up the lights in the dim hallway, "we have to economize now."

Just as he had at their first meeting, Rogers reminisced about his early experiences in the Oil Region. "It was a fabulous era," he said with a sigh, "and the story has never been told."

Ida was on the verge of asking him to let her write his memoirs of those historic days when they were interrupted by the arrival of another caller. Henry Rogers showed her to the door but he appeared eager to talk to her again. "Call my secretary in a week or ten days," he told her, "and we'll make an appointment." Ida called, but the appointment was never made. By then the United States Attorney General had instituted the suit aimed at dissolving the Standard Oil monopoly. Ida knew it would have been unwise for Henry Rogers to remain friends with the author of the book that had inspired the government's action.

For her first assignment for *The American* Ida suggested a series on the tariff. It was a subject that loomed as large in the public mind as the trusts had a few years earlier.

The tariff—a tax levied on goods imported from foreign countries—had started in the United States with the Constitution. In its simplest form, it was merely a device for raising money; but as the country grew and manufacturing increased, businessmen began pushing for a high tariff that would keep imported goods out and insure a monopoly for American products.

The opponents of the high tariff argued that the system led to too many abuses. All of the country's major industries had their own lobbyists in Washington. They were paid by manufacturers to influence congressmen to set high tariffs for goods that threatened to cut into the sales of their particular products. Bribes and lies were commonplace when the tariff schedules were being voted on, but in the long run, Ida believed, it was the consumer who was cheated. Without fear of foreign competition, American manufacturers were free to produce shoddy goods and sell them at exorbitant prices.

Ida agreed with the supporters of free trade, who held that each nation should be able to produce and export whatever products it was best at making. This would provide consumers with high-quality goods at the lowest possible prices.

One of Ida's most helpful advisers on the tariff series was former president Grover Cleveland, who had been a fierce opponent of the system. Ida had made Cleveland's acquaintance during her days at *McClure's,* when she was assigned the job of trying to persuade him to write his reminiscences. Although they had discussed the possibility at great length, in the end Cleveland declined to participate in what he laughingly called "the Tarbell-Cleveland fantasy."

Ida's series on the tariff did not inspire the sweeping reforms she had hoped for, but it earned her an invitation to become a member of a Tariff Commission that was organized by President Woodrow Wilson in 1916 to study the subject further. Her friend Jane Addams, the famous Chicago social worker, urged Ida to accept. Miss Addams was active in the movement for woman suffrage, and she felt the cause would be enhanced by having a woman on an important government committee. Ida declined the job. She was not a suffragette, nor did she feel qualified to serve on the Tariff Commission. It was not so impressive for a woman to get a job, she told Jane Addams, as it was for her to do it well.

Ida had always been skeptical of the suffragettes' cause. She resented their assertion that society would improve once women had a voice in government. She had learned from researching her first book, the life of Madame Roland, that women were no more enlightened in the field of politics than men.

She also objected to the feminists' tendency to belittle everything that women had accomplished in the past. To hear the suffragettes tell it, the American female had never been anything but a much-put-upon drudge.

Ida had tried to explode this myth many years before in her article on the patent office for *The Chautauquan*. Now she made a second attempt with a series of articles on women for *The American Magazine*. It included character studies of such bold and intelligent ladies of the past as President John Adams' wife, Abigail; the educator and writer, Catherine Beecher; and Mary Lyon, who founded Mount Holyoke, one of the country's first colleges for women. It was Ida's theory, based on her own experience, that a woman who had the ability and the determination to accomplish something could do it no matter what obstacles men put in her path.

More than anything else, however, Ida detested the suffragettes' militancy. She believed that women should have, and would eventually win, the vote, but she saw no need to be pushy or overbearing about asserting feminine rights.

In writing her series on tariffs for *The American* Ida charged that the industries that were protected by them did not always pass along their profits to their employees. Many workingmen were dreadfully underpaid. Ida had seen too many wretched homes and starving children to doubt it. This was not the case everywhere, however, and having shown the bad side of the picture, Ida felt that she should show the good side as well.

She spent four years traveling around the country visiting factories and factory towns. She met industrialists like Henry Ford of the Ford Motor Company, Elbert H. Gary of the United States Steel Corporation, and Owen D. Young of General Electric, and she was impressed with their efforts to give their employees fair wages and decent working conditions. Ida found in their policies a new sense of idealism that was a far cry from the greed and corruption of the old trusts. It prompted her to take a kindlier attitude toward the nation's businessmen.

In 1914 the owners of *The American Magazine* were faced with some grim facts. Publishing costs had risen so high that the profits on the magazine were beginning to decline. If *The American* was to keep going, more money would be needed to pay its way. There were dozens of long, solemn conferences in John Phillips' office before the editor-owners finally admitted that the financial burden would be too much for all of them. The following year they reluctantly sold *The American* to the Crowell Publishing Company. John Phillips was kept on as a consultant and director. John Siddall became the editor, but there was no place on the staff for Ida Tarbell.

She was then fifty-eight years old. A less energetic woman might have retired, but it never occurred to Ida to do anything but find another job. Louis Alber of the Coit Alber Lecture Bureau had been after her for some time to become a public speaker. Ida went to see him, and he immediately signed her up for the Chautauqua circuit. An outgrowth of the movement she had known as a girl, the circuit was a traveling assembly of lecturers and entertainers who appeared in various towns around the country. The meetings were held in a huge canvas tent with gaily colored pennants flying from the peaks. Tiers of wooden benches held the spectators, and the program included singers, dancers, and humorists, as well as serious lecturers like Ida.

No sooner had she signed the contract with the Coit Alber Lecture Bureau than Ida began to have doubts about the undertaking. Louis Alber had suggested she talk on "New Ideals in Business." Ida knew she could write a good speech about the subject, but could she deliver it? She was not a professional speaker. Maybe her voice wasn't strong enough to reach the tiers of listeners who filled the Chautauqua tents.

The would-be lecturer consulted a speech teacher. He confirmed her doubts and put her to work on a series of exercises designed to strengthen the muscles that controlled her voice. Ida had to spend several hours a day lying flat on her back with a pile of books on her diaphragm. Her instructions were to learn to breathe deeply enough so she could lift four or five volumes at a time. After weeks of practice, she finally succeeded. By the time the tour started in July, Ida's voice was strong enough to be heard in the farthest row of the Chautauqua tent.

Ida was scheduled to visit forty-nine towns in as many days. It meant dragging herself on and off trains, living out of a suitcase, putting up with drab hotel rooms and mediocre meals. Although she was relieved to get back to her Connecticut farmhouse, she had enjoyed the lecture tour, and after a few months' rest she was ready to take on another one.

It began in January 1917. She was still on the

road when the United States entered World War I in April.

Ida had always considered herself a pacifist. She hated war and believed that it created more problems than it solved. She lost faith in the pacifist movement, however, when the fighting began in Europe in 1914. The most outspoken advocates of peace were among the first to take up arms.

Ida knew the United States would inevitably be drawn into the war. When it was, she considered it her duty to do whatever she could to help. She preferred peace, but as she wrote later in her autobiography, "one simply must do what one can if the house is on fire."

A few days after Congress declared war, Ida was speaking at a dinner in a Cleveland hotel. Just before she was introduced a bellboy handed her a telegram. It was from President Woodrow Wilson, asking her to became a member of the Woman's Committee of the Council of National Defense. Ida concluded her lecture tour and canceled the contracts for two books she had been planning to write. By May 2 she was in Washington, D.C., working on ways to mobilize America's women for the war effort.

Chapter 16

Working with the Woman's Committee in Washington was a new experience for Ida. The head of the committee, Dr. Anna Shaw, was both a physician and an ordained minister; she was also one of the leaders of the woman suffrage movement. Ida was awed by her executive ability and by the efficiency with which she managed to set up branch offices of the Woman's Committee in every city in the country.

The offices served as information bureaus to tell women which of their services the government most needed. Usually the demand was for such traditionally feminine jobs as rolling bandages, knitting sweaters, or canning homegrown vegetables; but in some places women were also being called upon to work in factories as replacements for men who had gone to war.

The committee helped break down many of the barriers against employing women and saw to it that they were given fair wages and decent working conditions. Ida hoped to see its work continued after the war, and she suggested that it become a permanent branch of the Department of Labor. Dr. Anna Shaw rejected the idea. "If we can't have a separate department with a woman cabinet member at its head," she insisted, "we won't settle for anything else."

Ida never approved of Dr. Shaw's all-or-nothing attitude toward women's rights, and Dr. Shaw was impatient with Ida's insistence on discussing both sides of every question before forming an opinion about it. She accused her of talking too much and of being a "lukewarm person." After Ida cheerfully conceded that she might be right on both counts, the zealous feminist and the more objective writer managed to work together without difficulty. In the end, they became genuine friends.

Ida occasionally took time out from her committee work to lecture on the efforts that were being made in Washington to help bring the war to a speedy conclusion. She tried to be informative and matter-of-fact but she sometimes suspected that her audiences would have preferred a different type of speech. They wanted her to condemn Germany and to whip them into a fever of antagonism against the Germans.

Ida, who thought there was already too much hatred in the world, refused to stir up any more. She took such a dispassionate view of her country's enemy that one man who heard her speak came up to her afterward and accused her of being a pacifist. To prove it, he handed her a list of members of a peace society that Ida had joined before the war. At the top of the list was Jane Addams. "That woman," the man called her in disgust.

The founder of Hull House was an outspoken critic of America's entry into World War I. Ida did not agree with her stand, but she shared her horror of war and she had nothing but admiration for the work she was doing in Chicago's slums.

"I'm proud to be classed with 'that woman,' " Ida blazed, shoving the list back into the man's hand. "If there were more people in this world like Jane Addams, we wouldn't have this war in the first place."

World War I ended in November 1918. Ida finished up her work on the Woman's Committee by the end of the year and in January sailed for Europe. John Phillips, who had become editor of *Red Cross Magazine,* wanted her to write a series of articles on the organization's work in war-torn France.

Ida made her headquarters in Paris. At first she marveled at how well the city seemed to have survived the war. The longer she stayed, however, the more she realized that her first impression had been wrong. The great halls of the Louvre were bare. All the paintings and art treasures had been taken out and shipped to the south of France, where they would be safe from the German invaders. Many of the shops on the Left Bank were locked and shuttered. There was nothing to sell and nobody to buy.

One evening Ida went to visit Madame Marillier,

a Frenchwoman she had known when she first lived in Paris. The plaster in Madame Marillier's drawing room was chipped and peeling, and one of the doors was hanging from its hinges.

"Nothing has been mended in Paris for three years," her old friend told her sadly.

The greatest shock came when Madame Marillier handed her a list of Parisians who had been killed at the front. Many of the names were familiar to Ida. They were men she had laughed and talked with at Madame Marillier's dinner parties twenty-five years before.

The war had made its worst impact on the French countryside. There the landscape was littered with abandoned tanks and artillery; farmers trying to till their fields had to plow their way through discarded helmets, guns, and hand grenades.

Whole villages had been leveled by shellfire. In one place, Ida found a woman living in a basement under a pile of rubble that had once been her home. In another, the destruction was so complete that Ida watched a man and his wife trying to find the street where their house had been. They finally gave up and went away shaking their heads in bewilderment.

There were times when Ida was close to despair at the devastation and suffering she saw. But the French, with the help of a vast army of American relief workers, were determinedly rebuilding their shattered towns. One day Ida saw an old peasant woman weep with joy when a hen, brought by some of the Americans, laid its first egg. Soon after that, she walked across a deserted battlefield and found primroses blooming and a skylark singing overhead. For the first time in months, Ida's despair began to give way to hope.

For one who had known Paris in another era, it seemed strange now to find the city swarming with Americans. Ida in her Red Cross uniform was constantly being stopped on the street by doughboys. "Say Ma'am," the soldiers would ask, "would you help me pick out a souvenir for my girl?" Ida, an old hand at shopping in Paris, was happy to take them under her wing.

Many of the American faces she spied on the Place de la Concorde or the Rue de Rivoli were those of old friends. She met Auguste Jaccaci, the former art editor of *McClure's;* William Allen White, who had been a frequent contributor to both *McClure's* and the *American;* and her fellow editor, Ray Stannard Baker, who was now head of the American press delegation to the Paris peace conference. When they got together for lunch or dinner, Ida often felt she was back in New York.

After her series on the Red Cross was finished, John Phillips asked Ida to stay on and cover the peace talks in Paris. She followed every step of the long and confusing negotiations that finally led to the Treaty of Versailles. Although Ida did not approve of all the provisions of the treaty, she was heartily in favor of President Woodrow Wilson's proposal for the formation of a League of Nations. It was the first serious attempt by the nations of the world to put an end to war.

President Wilson returned to the United States and urged Congress to vote for America's participation in the League of Nations. The debate was already in progress when Ida came home and embarked on a ten weeks' tour with the Chautauqua circuit. Her topic was the League of Nations and what it could mean for world peace.

Woodrow Wilson's pleas fell on deaf ears. By the time Ida finished her tour, Congress was on the verge of ratifying the peace treaty but voting against the provision that would make the United States a member of the League of Nations. Ida heard the news with sorrow. With the League of Nations, there had been some chance of a permanent peace. Now she feared there was none at all.

Ida returned to her farmhouse in Bethel with a heavy heart, but it was hard to be depressed for long. The Connecticut countryside and the companionship of her friends and family soon cheered her up.

Ida's mother had died in 1917, and the old farm was now the Tarbell family home. Sarah had a small house on the property, and Will's daughter, Clara, lived in the guest cottage with her husband and their two small children. Will's older daughter, Esther, and his son, Scott, were regular visitors. Esther, in fact, had been married under the oak trees on the lawn.

Ida spent the next few weeks making plans for her future. She had no job, but she had decided to earn her living as a free-lance writer and lecturer. Above all, she wanted to find out more about a man she had studied many years before—Abraham Lincoln.

Lincoln had been in Ida's thoughts all during World War I. He was one of the few leaders in history who had made an honest effort to understand the men and the situations he dealt with. If more people followed his example, Ida was convinced, there might be a chance for countries to live together in harmony. She vowed to take advantage of every opportunity she could find to write and talk about Abraham Lincoln. It would be her contribution to the cause of peace.

Chapter 17

In the course of the next twenty years Ida Tarbell wrote five more books about Abraham Lincoln and dozens of magazine articles. When she went on a lecture tour, it was scheduled for the weeks around February 12, and the topic, again, was Lincoln.

Until Ida came along, the nation's Civil War president had generally been portrayed as either a dull historical figure or an unreal saint. Ida made him both lively and human. Many historians give her the credit for turning Abraham Lincoln into the beloved figure he is today.

Ida's semiretirement in Connecticut was interrupted by several long visits to Washington, D.C. In 1919 President Woodrow Wilson asked her to serve on a committee to study ways in which employers and employees could work out their differences without resorting to strikes and violence. Ida found it a disheartening experience.

The United States was being attacked by an epidemic of labor troubles that had begun soon after the end of World War I. It started with a strike of New York harbor workers in January 1919. After that, the railroad workers, the cigar makers, the garment workers, and even the actors walked off their jobs. In Boston the police went on strike and threw the city into chaos; but the biggest and bitterest dispute occurred when members of the American Federation of Labor called a nationwide strike against the United States Steel Corporation.

The strike was still in progress when Woodrow Wilson organized his Industrial Conference in the fall of 1919. Ida was one of four women who participated. The other members—some fifty in all—included Elbert H. Gary, chairman of the board of the U.S. Steel Corporation; Dr. Charles Eliot, the distinguished former president of Harvard; Samuel Gompers, who had organized the American Federation of Labor; and John D. Rockefeller, Jr.

Ida was not sure how to behave toward the son of the man she had portrayed as the king of the robber barons. John D. Rockefeller, Jr., was equally nervous at the thought of meeting the "Terror of the Trusts." Their mutual friend William Allen White advised Rockefeller to be calm and natural. Ida acted the same way, and there were no awkward moments even when they found themselves seated next to each other at a formal dinner one evening.

The announcement of President Wilson's Industrial Conference brought a warm response from the public, and Ida had high hopes its members might actually come up with a document that would settle the differences between labor and management. The conference had no sooner convened, however, than Samuel Gompers insisted that they appoint a subcommittee to report on the strike against U.S. Steel. Dr. Eliot objected and reminded the members that they were there not to settle present disputes but to discover how to avoid future ones.

The mere mention of the steel strike aroused the animosities of both the labor leaders and the industrialists. Even when they finally got down to business, they were never able to agree on how the unions should operate and what their bargaining rights should be. There was hostility and suspicion on both sides, and in the end the labor men walked out. President Wilson was forced to disband the conference and nothing was accomplished.

Ida's next experience with committee work occurred in 1921, when President Warren G. Harding named her to another commission to study the problems of unemployment that had arisen after the war. Again there was hostility between labor and management, but this time they managed to overcome their differences.

They drew up what, in Ida's opinion, was an excellent plan for coping with the periodic business slumps that had always been an inescapable factor in the American economy. When the postwar depression disappeared and was followed by a period of prosperity during the 1920's, the government lost all interest in the problem. Ida always thought that if the committee's proposals had been put into action, the country might have avoided the disastrous depression that began in 1929.

All during the years that the government's case against the Standard Oil monopoly was being tried in the courts, Ida had been deluged with offers from magazines and newspapers to write about the proceedings. She refused them all. Someday, perhaps, she might go back and study the trials, but for the time being she had had more than her fill of John D. Rockefeller and his company.

After the Supreme Court decision in 1911, George Wickersham, the United States Attorney General who initiated the suit, advised Ida to wait at least ten years before writing anything more about Standard Oil. It would take that long to evaluate the decision's effects. Ida agreed. By then she might be more in the mood to add a third volume to her epic history.

Ten years passed, and Ida still could not manage to find either the time or the desire to bring *The History of the Standard Oil Company* up to date. She put it off again and again and probably would have given it up completely had Samuel S. McClure not suddenly reappeared in her life.

Both McClure and his magazine had had their financial ups and downs since Ida severed her relationship with them in 1906. The magazine had suspended publication for several years, but in 1922 it was revived, with McClure in the editor's chair. One of the first things he wanted to publish was an updated version of Ida's successful series from the past.

Ida took the train down from Bethel to see her old friend and to discuss the new volume. As she listened to McClure, she was reminded of the first time she had met him in Paris. He still bubbled over with the same gaiety and excitement. It was going to be fun working for him again. She also liked the prospect of helping to bring the old *McClure's* back to life.

Ida was in the midst of working on the third volume of her history when she received word that S. S. McClure was again in financial hot water. The magazine would be forced to suspend publication once more. She put the series aside with no regrets. She knew she would never finish it, but the whole story was too far in the past for her to care. She had other, more current, topics to write about.

In 1925 an editor approached her with an idea for a biography of Elbert H. Gary, the lawyer and former county judge who was chairman of the board of directors of the United States Steel Corporation. Ida had written about Judge Gary in *The American Magazine* many years before and had praised him for giving high wages to his employees, looking after their safety and health, and offering them shares in the company's stock.

United States Steel, however, was for all practical purposes a monopoly, and in some circles Elbert Gary was considered as much of a villain as John D. Rockefeller. Ida had misgivings about writing his biography. Suppose the rumors about Elbert Gary proved to be true? She would feel bound in conscience to report them.

Before signing the contract for the book, Ida went to Judge Gary and told him bluntly that although she admired him as a humanitarian, she had heard questionable stories about his ethics. Gary nodded. U. S. Steel had already been investigated by several government agencies, he told her. None of them had uncovered anything illegal. "Now it's your turn," the judge told her. "If you can find anything wrong in our doings, I want to be the first to know it."

Ida began the biography with the same understanding she had made with Henry Rogers. It was to be her book, and her judgment must prevail.

Ida's judgment, however, proved to be much less critical than it had been in the past. Judge Gary had never stooped to the unscrupulous methods that John D. Rockefeller had used in organizing the Standard Oil Company. He was a lawyer and he always stayed within the law; but he was definitely not the hero that Ida portrayed. She glossed over the fact that U. S. Steel was a virtual monopoly, and she also failed to mention Gary's role in the famous steel strike of 1919.

When the workers went on strike for an eight-hour day and the recognition of their union by the company, Judge Gary rejected their demands and refused to meet with union officials for any further discussions. The company's total lack of sympathy for its striking employees subsequently led to several acts of violence. In a plant in New Castle, Pennsylvania, mill guards shot five strikers, and in Buffalo, New York, two men were killed and fifty wounded.

When Ida's biography of Elbert H. Gary came out, many people accused her of whitewashing the judge and his company. One newspaper said the book should be called *The Taming of Ida M. Tarbell* and bemoaned the fact that she had betrayed her reputation for hardheaded reporting.

Ida was not surprised at the attacks. She always said that writing Judge Gary's biography was one of the bravest acts of her career. Sometimes it took more courage to say good things about a man than bad ones.

In some ways she was right. Judge Gary had accomplished many reforms in industry and was rarely given credit for them. But although his reputation was often unjustly smeared, it was inaccurate to depict him as a man without faults.

The explanation for Ida's laudatory biography may be that she worked too closely with the judge in preparing it and that her reporter's objectivity collapsed in the face of a personal relationship. Ida was too kindhearted not to want to believe the best of anyone she considered a friend.

Chapter 18

In 1930 Ida celebrated her seventy-third birthday.
She was grateful that she could face her old age with
a minimum of financial worries. After she had
scored her initial success with her life of Napoleon,
she was able to command prices of $2,000 or $3,000
apiece for her articles. She earned almost $50,000
for her series on the Standard Oil Company in
McClure's, and there was even more money when
the installments were published as a book. There
were royalties from her other books as well, and her
lecture fees usually came to $1,000 each.

Ida, who lived simply, was able to put aside most
of her earnings. The income from her savings and
investments helped support her in her later years.

In addition to her many studies of Abraham Lincoln, Ida also wrote a biography of Owen D. Young,
the chairman of the General Electric Company, that
was published in 1932. In 1936 she completed a
study of American business from 1878 to 1898 for

the impressive thirteen-volume *History of American Life* that was edited by the noted Harvard historian, Arthur Schlesinger. Three years later her autobiography, *All in the Day's Work,* appeared.

McClure's Magazine had been given another lease on life in 1925. It collapsed again in less than a year and was sold to the millionaire publisher William Randolph Hearst. It limped along for a few years as a cheap movie magazine, then a men's magazine, and finally disappeared completely in 1930.

Samuel McClure, his career as an editor finished, tried several other ventures. None of them were successful, and in 1934 he took a room at the Murray Hill Hotel in New York and retired to write the story of his life.

McClure still kept in touch with his old friends. In 1936 he invited Ida, John Phillips, and the magazine's former fiction editor, Viola Roseboro, to join him in celebrating his seventy-ninth birthday. The four septuagenarians had to exchange almost fifty letters before they finally found a date on which they were all free. By then McClure's birthday was three months past, but they had a festive lunch at the Union League Club and chatted happily about old times.

Ida saw Samuel McClure for the last time in 1941, when his daughter brought him to visit her in Bethel. He seemed frail and shaky. "I felt like I was saying good-bye to a dying man," she wrote to John Phillips when he left.

Ironically, Ida, who seemed so strong and healthy,

died first. She was busy right up until the end. In addition to her writing, she served as president of the Pen and Brush Club, an organization of women artists and writers that she had founded in 1913. She made several trips around the country and spent two winters in Tucson working on a new magazine about the southwest and lecturing at the University of Arizona.

Ida celebrated her eighty-sixth birthday on November 5, 1943. A few weeks later she was stricken with pneumonia. She remained at her Connecticut farmhouse until after Christmas. Then the doctor decided to move her to a hospital in Bridgeport. She died there on the morning of January 6, 1944, with her sister Sarah at her bedside.

Much as Ida loved Bethel, she had asked to be buried in the state of her birth. Her body was interred in Connecticut for the winter, and when spring came it was moved to Titusville and buried in Woodlawn Cemetery beside her mother and father, and her brother Will, who had died a few years before.

Ida left her Connecticut home to her sister Sarah and her books and papers to the Allegheny College library. Her estate was divided equally between Sarah, her sister-in-law, Ella Scott Tarbell, and her two nieces Esther and Clara.

After her death, Ida was eulogized all over the country. One newspaper editorial compared her to her favorite hero, Abraham Lincoln. "She was as honest and kindly and thoroughly American, in the

161

loftiest sense, as he was," it said. "He would have understood her as she did him."

But of the dozens of books and articles she wrote, Ida Tarbell is still remembered for *The History of the Standard Oil Company*. It brought her fame as a writer and as a reformer, and won her a lasting place in American history as the first and best of the muckrakers.

Bibliography

Baker, Ray Stannard. *American Chronicle*. New York: Charles Scribner's Sons, 1945.

Chalmers, David Mark. *The Social and Political Ideas of the Muckrakers*. New York: The Citadel Press, 1964.

Filler, Louis. *Crusaders for American Liberalism*. New York: Harcourt, Brace, 1932.

Josephson, Matthew. *The Robber Barons*. New York: A Harvest Book, Harcourt, Brace & World, Inc., 1962.

Lyon, Peter. *Success Story! The Life and Times of S. S. McClure*. Deland, Fla.: Everett Edwards, Inc. 1967.

Myers, Gustavus. *History of the Great American Fortunes*. New York: The Modern Library, 1936.

Steffens, Lincoln. *Autobiography*. New York: Harcourt, Brace, 1931.

Sullivan, Mark. *Our Times*. New York: Charles Scribner's Sons, 1933.

Swados, Harvey. *Years of Conscience: The Muck-rakers*. Cleveland and New York: Meridian Books, The World Publishing Company, 1962.

Tarbell, Ida M. *All in the Day's Work*. New York: The Macmillan Company, 1939.

————. *The History of the Standard Oil Company*, edited by David M. Chalmers. New York: Harper Torchbooks, Harper & Row, Publishers, 1966.

————. *The Life of Elbert H. Gary*. New York: D. Appleton, 1925.

Weinberg, Arthur and Lila, eds. *The Muckrakers*. New York: Capricorn Books, 1961.

Index

Adams, Abigail, 141
Adams, John, 141
Adams, Samuel Hopkins, 126
Addams, Jane, 140, 147
Alber, Louis, 142-143
Allegheny College, 25-30, 36, 38, 41, 54, 78, 161
All in the Day's Work (Tarbell, 1939), 160
American Magazine, 134-136, 139, 141-142, 149, 156
American Protective Association, 78
Atlantic Monthly, 50, 114
Attorney General, U.S., 124, 138, 155
Autobiography of Lincoln Steffens, 83

Baker, Ray Stannard, 81-82, 86, 125, 127, 132, 149
Beecher, Catherine, 141
Bell, Alexander Graham, 28, 77
Bissell, George, 4

Bonaparte, Charles, 61
Bonaparte, Napoleon, *see* Napoleon Bonaparte
Boyden, Albert, 132, 135
Buffalo Lubricating Works, 104
Bugbee, Dr. Lucius, 25-26, 36
Burlingame, Edward, 46-47
business corruption, 1, 20-22, 79, 85-87, 99, 101-104, 108-109, 112-117, 124-125, 136, 139
Bureau of Corporations, U.S., 124

Carnegie, Andrew, 22
Century Magazine, 50, 65, 76, 82, 136
Chautauqua Assembly, 37, 40
Chautauqua circuit, 142-143, 150
Chautauqua Literary and Scientific Circle, 37
Chautauqua Movement, 36, 142

Chautauquan, 36-42, 44, 45, 56, 87, 101, 141

Chicago *Tribune,* 46, 70

Cincinnati *Times-Star,* 46

Civil War, U.S., 7, 10, 73-75, 152

Cleveland, Grover, 139-140

Coit Alber Lecture Bureau, 142-143

Collier's, 126

Commerce and Labor, U.S. Department of, 124

Congress, U.S., 126, 150
  business investigations by, 21, 99
  lobbyists' influence on, 78, 86, 126, 139

copper industry, 137

Cornell University, 25-26

Cosmopolitan, 126

Daily Herald (Chautauqua), 40

Dana, Charles A., 72-76

Douglas, Stephen, 69, 75

Drake, Edwin, 3, 4, 107

economy, U.S. (*see also* panic of 1857, of 1893, of 1907), 154-155

Erie Railroad, 102

Everybody's Magazine, 137

Flood, Dr. Theodore, 36, 38, 42, 48

Ford, Henry, 141

Ford Motor Company, 141

Frank Leslie's Illustrated Monthly, 134

Gary, Elbert H., 141, 153, 156-158

General Electric Company, 141, 159

Gilder, Jeanette, 136

Gilder, Richard Watson, 76, 82-83, 136

Gompers, Samuel, 153-154

Gould, Jay, 23

government corruption:
  federal, 79
  municipal, 81, 85, 125

Grant, Ulysses S., 74

Grayson, David, *see* Baker, Ray Stannard

Harding, Warren G., 154

Harper's, 10, 50, 114

Harriman, Edward, 23

Haskins, George, 28-29

Hasse, Adelaide, 100

Hay, John, 65-66

Hearst, William Randolph, 160

Hepburn Act, 125

Herndon, William, 66, 69

Hess, Ida, 9, 13

Hill, James, 23

History of American Life (Schlesinger, ed.), 160

History of the Standard Oil Company (Tarbell, 1904), 1, 89, 105, 111, 119, 121-123, 125, 128, 155, 162

Hoar, George Frisbie, 78-79

Hubbard, Mr. and Mrs. Gardiner Green, 59-61, 67, 75, 77

Industrial Conference (Wilson's, 1919), 153
industrial workers, 39, 141-142, 156
industry, *see* business corruption; copper industry; labor unions; oil industry; steel industry; sugar trust

Jungle, The (Sinclair), 126

labor unions, 39, 85, 125, 152-154, 157-158
Langley, Dr. Samuel Pierpoint, 77-78
Lawson, Thomas, 137
League of Nations, 150
Lee, Ivy, 123
legislatures, state, business investigations by, 21, 99
Library of Congress, 59, 79
Life of Abraham Lincoln (Tarbell, 1900, book based on articles), 72, 75
Lincoln, Abraham, 8, 65-72, 75, 100, 151, 152, 159, 161
Lincoln, Mary Todd, 69
Lincoln, Robert, 67-68, 75
lobbyists, 78, 86, 126, 139
Lyon, Mary, 141
Lyons, Emily, 67

Madame Roland: A Biographical Study (Tarbell, 1896), 41-42, 47, 57, 61-62, 140
magazines, U.S.: 10, 36-42, 44-48, 50, 54-55, 57-59, 61, 63-65, 68, 71, 73-78, 81-87,

magazines, U.S. (*cont.*)
99, 101, 105, 111-112, 114-116, 119, 128, 131-136, 141-142, 147, 149, 155-156, 159-160
"Golden Age" of, 84
muckraking by, 81, 105, 111, 119, 122, 125-127, 137, 139-140
sensationalism by, 126-127
Mahaffy, Dr. J. P., 40
McClure, Samuel S., 50-51, 54-55, 58-61, 63-66, 71, 73, 76-78, 81-83, 85-88, 100-101, 105, 111-112, 128, 131-132, 155-156, 160
McClure's Magazine, 1, 54-55, 57-59, 61, 63-64, 68, 71, 73-78, 81-87, 101, 124, 131-133, 134, 149, 155-156, 159, 160
muckraking by, 81, 105, 111, 119, 122, 125
McClure's Universal Journal, 132
McClure Syndicate, 48
Medill, Joseph, 70-71
Methodist Church, 25, 29, 36-37, 58
monopolies, *see* business corruption
Morgan, John Pierpont, 22, 85
muckraking, 125-127

Napoleon Bonaparte (*see also Short Life of Napoleon Bonaparte*), 58-62, 64, 100, 159

New York Central Railroad, 102

New York *Sun*, 72, 74

New York Tribune, 10

Nicolay, John, 65-66

oil industry, U.S.:
    in California, 86
    in Kansas, 128-129
    in Oklahoma, 129-130
    in Pennsylvania, 3-4, 7, 14,
        19-21, 87, 129
    Standard Oil monopoly of,
        1, 40, 86-87, 99, 101-104, 109,
        114-116, 118, 122, 138
*Owen D. Young—A New Type
    of Industrial Leader* (Tar-
    bell, 1932), 159

panic of 1857, 2

panic of 1893, 55, 58, 105, 120

panic of 1907, 137

Pasteur, Louis, 54-55

patent holders, women, 39, 141

Pen and Brush Club, 161

Pennsylvania Oil Region, 1, 3-
    5, 7, 14, 19-22, 26, 40, 87,
    101, 107-108, 135, 138

Pennsylvania Railroad, 102

Perry, Leslie, 73-74

Petroleum Producers' Union,
    20-21

Phillips, David Graham, 126

Phillips, John S., 63-65, 73, 78,
    82-83, 88, 121, 131-133, 137,
    142, 147, 149, 160

Pittsburgh *Dispatch*, 46

Poland Union Seminary, 30-35

railroads, 19, 22, 23, 114-115
    "drawbacks" by, 102-103
    rebates by, 20-21, 101-103,
        109, 113, 124-125

Recollections of the Civil War
    (Dana), 72, 75

Red Cross Magazine, 147-149

Reminiscences (Schurz), 75

"robber barons," 22

Rockefeller, Frank, 119-121

Rockefeller, John D., 21-22,
    101-105, 108-110, 117-121,
    122-124, 155-157

Rockefeller, John D., Jr., 153

Rogers, Henry, 105-110, 112-114,
    116-117, 136-138, 157

Roland, Mme. Jeanne Manon
    Phlipon, 41-42, 47, 57,
    61-62, 140

Roosevelt, Theodore, 124, 126-
    127

Roseboro, Viola, 160

Rouseville, Pa., 12-15, 107-108

Schlesinger, Arthur, 160

Schurz, Carl, 75-76

Scribner's, publishers, 47, 61

Scribner's Magazine, 46-47, 50

Shame of the Cities, The (Stef-
    fens), 81

Shaw, Dr. Anna, 145-146

Sherman Anti-Trust Act, 125

*Short Life of Napoleon Bona-
    parte* (Tarbell, 1895), 61-
    62, 64, 75, 159

Siddall, John, 101, 103, 118-
    119, 120, 132, 142

Sinclair, Upton, 126

Smithsonian Institution, 77, 79

South Improvement Company, 20-21, 39-40, 87, 101-102, 108

Spanish-American War, 81

Standard Oil Company (see also *History of the Standard Oil Company*), 21, 40, 86-87, 90-106, 108-111, 113-117, 119-120, 123-125, 157, 159
  lawsuits against, 99, 110, 114, 116, 124-125, 138, 155
  sabotage by, 104, 114-117

State Department, U.S., 59

steel industry, 22, 86

Steffens, Lincoln, 81-83, 125, 132

stock market, 113-114, 137

sugar trust, 86

Supreme Court, U.S., 1, 125, 155

Tarbell, Clara, 150, 161

Tarbell, Ella Scott, 58, 136, 161

Tarbell, Esther, 150, 161

Tarbell, Esther McCullogh, 2-3, 5-6, 8-9, 11-13, 18-19, 24, 25, 36, 43, 58, 136, 150, 161

Tarbell, Franklin, 2-6, 8-13, 15, 18-19, 21-22, 25, 36, 43, 58, 107, 113, 119, 128, 161

Tarbell, Franklin, Jr., 9

Tarbell, Ida Minerva:
  as biographer, 41-42, 47, 57, 58-62, 64-71, 156-159
  birth of (1857), 1-2
  childhood of, 2-3, 5-19

Tarbell, Ida Minerva (*cont.*)
  as committee member, 144-147, 152-154
  death of (1944), 160-161
  education of, 15-18, 25-30, 41
  as free-lance writer, 42, 46-48, 54-55, 63, 151-152
  as journalist, 38-42, 63-78, 82-83, 85-142
  as lecturer, 142-143, 146, 150-152, 159, 161
  as muckraker, 1, 122-127, 139-140
  pacifism of, 144, 146-147, 150-151
  in Paris, 42-58, 147-150
  science, interest in, 7, 16-18, 23-24, 27-28, 30, 34, 41, 54
  social problems, awareness of, 22-23, 39-40, 79-80, 84-85
  as teacher, 30-36
  woman suffrage movement, opinion of, 39, 41, 140-141
  works by, *see* individual titles; *History of American Life*

Tarbell, Sarah, 9, 11, 13, 18-19, 136, 150, 161

Tarbell, Scott, 150

Tarbell, William, 5, 7, 9-11, 13, 18-19, 29, 53, 58, 87, 136, 150, 161

tariffs, U.S., 86, 139-141

Tingley, Jeremiah, 27-28, 78

Titusville, Pa., 3, 13-15, 17-19, 20-21, 36, 52-53, 58, 113, 161

trusts, *see* business corruption

Twain, Mark, 105-106

U.S. Steel Corporation, 85, 141, 153, 156-157

Vacuum Oil Company, 103-104
Vanderbilt, Cornelius, 23

White, William Allen, 149, 153
Whitney, Henry C., 70-71
Wilson, Woodrow, 68, 81, 140, 149-150, 152-154
Woman's Committee of Council of National Defense, 144-147

woman suffrage movement, 39, 140-141, 145-146
women:
  employment of, 82-83, 145-146
  higher education of, 26-27, 141
World War I, 144-148, 151

Young, Owen D., 141, 159

About the Author

Alice Fleming says that she is enough of a feminist to enjoy seeing a woman succeed in a man's world. She has also enjoyed writing about such women; her previous book in the Women of America series was a biography of Margaret Chase Smith, *The Senator from Maine,* and she has told the stories of famous women doctors and teachers in other books.

Mrs. Fleming was born in New Haven, Connecticut, and grew up there and in Yonkers, New York. She was graduated from Trinity College in Washington, D.C., and later took a master's degree at Columbia University. With her husband, the writer Thomas J. Fleming, and her four children, she now lives in New York City and devotes most of her time to writing.